Broadband Network Technology

An Overview for the Data and Telecommunications Industries

By Edward Cooper

Sytek, Inc.
Mountain View, California

Sytek

Sytek Press
1225 Charleston Road
Mountain View, California 94043

Prentice-Hall, Inc.
Englewood Cliffs, New Jersey 07632

International Standard Book
    Number: ISBN 0-13-083379-7

Editor: Christopher L. Poda
Book Design:
    Richard Klein Design, Inc.
Editorial/Production Supervision:
    Diana Drew
Cover Illustration: Robert Pleasure
Interior Illustrations: Gemini Graphics
Text Typesetting: George Graphics
Manufacturing Buyer: Ed O'Dougherty

This 1986 edition published by
Prentice-Hall, Inc.
A Division of Simon & Schuster
Englewood Cliffs, New Jersey 07632

Printed in the United States of
    America

10 9 8 7 6 5 4 3 2 1

ISBN 0-13-083379-7 025

Prentice-Hall International (UK) Limited,
    London
Prentice-Hall of Australia Pty. Limited,
    Sydney
Prentice-Hall Canada Inc., *Toronto*
Prentice-Hall Hispanoamericana, S.A.,
    Mexico
Prentice-Hall of India Private Limited,
    New Delhi
Prentice-Hall of Japan, Inc., *Tokyo*
Prentice-Hall of Southeast Asia Pte. Ltd.,
    Singapore
Editora Prentice-Hall do Brasil, Ltda.,
    Rio de Janeiro
Whitehall Books Limited,
    Wellington, New Zealand

Preface

During the 1970s, advances in microelectronics led to the development of small, powerful electronic workstations and personal computers. As hardware prices dropped and versatile applications software became available, many individuals and organizations began buying and using these systems. At the same time, corporate electronic data processing departments made remote access to their centralized computers possible by distributing terminals and other input/output devices throughout the company's offices.

The problem of connecting many terminals, printers, and other remote peripheral devices to a large, centralized computer was solved by using point-to-point multiconductor cables, modems with telephone lines, and even dedicated coaxial cables. These techniques led to wiring mazes and maintenance problems in even medium-sized plants and office buildings. A better solution to the interconnection problem was developed by combining the technologies of broadband cable communications and programmable microprocessor and interface circuits. This same approach was also used to connect separate personal computers and workstations together into local area networks (LANs). Broadband networking allows many different devices to be connected throughout a large area with a single cable.

Broadband radio frequency (RF) coaxial cable systems have been in service since the 1950s. The designs, components, and tools for such systems have been developed and refined by several different companies. Mass production has lowered the cost of broadband cable components greatly. Similarly, the cost of intelligent interface devices has dropped because of continuing advances in the semiconductor industry.

Broadband local area networks can now be used to link sophisticated data processing equipment, and can provide a reliable communication backbone for transmitting audio and video signals throughout a facility. Data transmission became practical with the development of the RF modem, which translates digital data into RF signals and vice versa. A packet communication unit that combines an RF modem with a standard RS-232 interface port permits data transfer among digital devices from many different vendors.

This book will help managers, engineers, and operators involved with data communications to understand the principles and techniques of broadband networks. It will provide readers with the knowledge and vocabulary necessary to communicate effectively with broadband consultants and equipment vendors. The reader will gain an understanding of the capabilities and limitations of the broadband approach, and of the job of the broadband system designer. This should ease the task of working with specialists to design the best network for your application.

This book is not intended to be a comprehensive reference on broadband communications, or to be the definitive tutorial on broadband system design. RF system design is learned through years of experience in designing networks, and not by reading books.

Readers desiring to gain an overview of broadband communications should begin with chapter one. Technical personnel might skim over the first chapter, read chapters two and three, and concentrate on the detailed information in chapters four, five, and six.

Chapter one provides general information on the development of broadband systems and their applications, especially in local area networks.

Chapter two discusses several topics that are important in understanding broadband networks.

Chapter three contains details regarding different cable system architectures that are currently used, including a comparison of single and dual cable systems.

Chapter four describes characteristics of the active and passive components that comprise broadband networks.

Chapter five covers system-level design problems that must be solved for each network. Sample calculations show how various design factors interact with each other.

Chapter six includes details on system alignment procedures, common problems that can occur, and possible solutions to these problems.

Chapter seven lists sources of further information.

The appendices following the text contain specific references to terms and symbols, CATV system frequencies, tools and test equipment, equipment manufacturers, and books in the field. Details of RF calculations and system grounding are also included.

For additional information consult the reference materials listed. To discuss your specific requirements please call the Cable Design and Consulting Group of Sytek, Inc., Mountain View, California (415/966-7347). In addition, we hope to continue to provide informative overviews, such as this one, in other areas of broadband communications.

We would like to thank the many people who contributed their time and knowledge in making this book. In particular, Linda, Richard, and Cheralynn Cooper, who had to put up with Ed's typing on a terminal for several weeks. Christopher's parents, Louis and Josephine Poda, have provided support and encouragement which is greatly appreciated.

Mike Pliner of Sytek provided the necessary support for the extensive effort that was required. Several other individuals provided suggestions on the format and technical content: Helmut Hess and Cecil Turner of the RF Systems Division of General Instrument Corporation; Ken Howell of TRW; and Marcia Allen, Mike Kalashian, Peter Filice, and Don Koller of Sytek, Incorporated. Ralph DeMent of DEC, and all our professional contacts encouraged us to write this overview. Allen Day, Susan Lindsay, and Michele Bisson were very helpful in the design and production process.

Welcome to the world of broadband communications!

Edward B. Cooper, author
Christopher L. Poda, editor

Contents

Contents

Contents

Figures

Tables

Background and Applications

Introduction

Over the past decade, electronic data communication requirements have exceeded the capacities and capabilities of existing telephone, twisted pair, and similar communication media. Continuing advances in data processing, new developments in interactive equipment, and expanding network implementations impose further strains on conventional wiring schemes. Techniques using standard twisted pairs are cumbersome when the system requires:

▶ Frequent expansion or reconfiguration

▶ Complex central intelligence

▶ Flexible equipment placement and data flow

In addition, these techniques cannot distribute real time, high quality video signals for video conferencing and security applications. The *office of the future* and *the wired city* concepts would require multiple, overlaying wiring schemes, if they were to be implemented using conventional wiring.

The problems faced by many facility managers are further compounded by the complex wiring necessary to provide each building with contemporary systems for communication (voice, video, and data), emergency detection and warning, and equipment control. As a result, ceilings bulge from the weight of many twisted wire cables, telephone lines, and dedicated coaxial cables installed to provide current and future services.

Fortunately, advances in cable television technology have led to the development of a multimode broadband signal distribution technique. This technique requires only a single coaxial cable to carry many different signals simultaneously. A broadband local area network (LAN) provides reliable, inexpensive, wideband communications within a single building or throughout a dispersed site such as a campus or an industrial park.

This chapter discusses broadband communications in general, including its origins and applications.

Broadband Communications

Broadband is a generic term that refers to a type of wide bandwidth communication network. Some of the main characteristics of a broadband network are listed below and briefly described in the following sections.

▶ A broadband network is a *communications utility* that can be used by many different services; it provides the backbone for an integrated information system throughout the area it serves.

▶ Information signals modulate *RF carrier signals* that are transported by *coaxial cable*.

▶ Many different types of information signals can share the cable's wide bandwidth (several hundred megahertz) by *frequency division multiplexing* (*FDM*).

▶ Each FDM channel can be *subdivided* further by using a variety of channel access techniques, such as time-division multiplexing (TDM).

▶ The network is *geographically independent*: devices can be attached to the network anywhere and operate correctly.

▶ The network is *robust*. The failure of an interface device attached to the network cannot prevent the entire system from operating.

One early application of broadband communications was to provide television signals to remote areas via coaxial cable. The components and network design principles developed for these cable television systems have been directly applied to broadband local area networks.

The CATV Connection

Community Antenna Television (CATV) systems began operation in 1949. The CATV operator built an antenna site and a coaxial cable distribution network. The antenna site received distant broadcast television signals. The cable distribution network connected the antenna site (or a separate signal distribution facility) to each customer's house. Television signals were received, processed, and transmitted along the cables to viewers. Cable transmission was used in locations that could not receive broadcast transmissions directly because of distance or because of interfering buildings or terrain.

These early systems were limited in the services and signal quality they provided. Many system operators were satisfied if they could receive, amplify, and deliver a signal to locations where it could not be received directly. Since most television viewers were within reception range of at least one broadcast station, CATV systems were confined to serving small, remote areas of the country.

In the past decade the CATV industry has grown greatly. Operators attracted new customers by offering additional channels and new services that were not available from broadcast television stations. In 1982, the cable television industry served 21 million subscribers. By the end of 1989 that figure is predicted to rise to 65 million (more than thirty percent penetration of the available market). This potential customer base encourages greater investment in new technologies. New research and development will bring lower equipment costs and more services to both CATV and broadband local area networks.

In this overview, the terms CATV and broadband are used synonymously. Both systems use identical equipment and similar system designs. In general, CATV systems extend over a wide area (often city-wide), and are franchised operations. Broadband networks extend over a limited area (one or more buildings), and are privately owned. Furthermore, broadband networks are usually bidirectional. CATV systems are primarily unidirectional, although two-way transmission capability is becoming more popular. Bidirectional CATV systems can supply customers with additional services, such as data communications and interactive videotext.

Coaxial Cable

As a signal distribution medium, coaxial cables are reliable, economical, and can be installed in existing conduits, underground cableways, and plenums. Coaxial cables are available in several types, suitable to various environmental conditions. If damaged or broken, the cable can be spliced or short sections can be replaced quickly by semi-skilled personnel using simple tools.

Coaxial cables provide excellent shielding from electromagnetic interference (EMI) and radio frequency interference (RFI). They are ideal for use in electrically noisy industrial environments, where twisted pair wires are difficult to use effectively.

Fault isolation in a coaxial network is straightforward using readily available test equipment. The isolation process can be enhanced by automated statistical recall systems, status monitoring facilities, and programmable spectrum analyzers and signal generators.

Frequency Multiplexing

Frequency multiplexing permits simultaneous use of the cable by many different services. The large bandwidth available on the cable is divided into channels, usually 6 MHz wide. One channel can be used for transmitting video from a local camera, while another channel can carry data between a computer and a terminal. These applications can be totally independent yet use the same cable as their communication medium.

The following list mentions some typical applications that can share a single broadband local area network. Some require only one-way communication and others require a two-way capability. Careful planning of equipment to be purchased and frequency assignments to be made is necessary to ensure proper operation and no spectrum conflicts. Figure 1-1 depicts a broadband network connecting all the buildings inside a single facility. Figure 1-2 shows some of the services that could use this network.

▶ Data communications

▶ Broadcast television signal distribution

▶ Video conferencing

▶ Security and safety monitoring
   ▷ Fire alarms
   ▷ Intrusion alarms
   ▷ Closed circuit television (CCTV) surveillance cameras
   ▷ Remote television camera control
   ▷ Building and area access control

▶ Paging

▶ Energy management

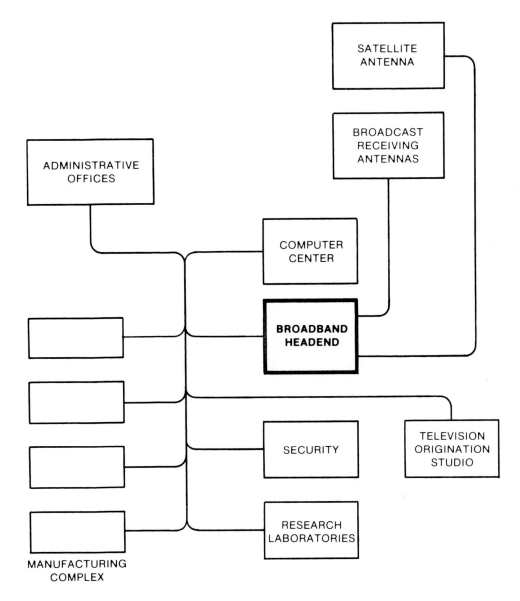

Figure 1-1. Broadband Coaxial Network in a Dispersed Facility

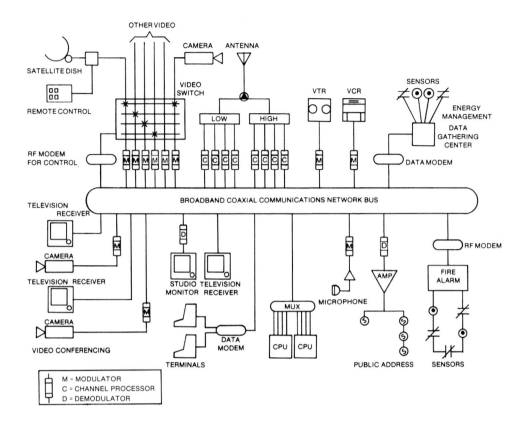

Figure 1-2. Multiple Services Using a Broadband Network

Geographic Independence

Geographic independence means that a device performs as specified regardless of where it resides in the network. When a building is fully wired with coaxial cable, devices can be attached anywhere a standard outlet has been installed. This allows, for example, a data communication user to disconnect an interface unit, move to a different office, reconnect the device to the cable outlet, and resume working with no need for additional wiring changes.

The cost of conventional wiring to provide an equivalent, multiservice capability with the same flexibility would be much greater than that of a single coaxial cable. For each of the services to be provided, the conventional scheme would require many dedicated wires and cables throughout the building, some overlapping others. With broadband, any type of device for any type of service could be placed wherever the single coaxial cable was accessible. A complex color television camera, a simple smoke detector, and many other devices connect to the same coaxial information utility line.

The Business Community

Broadband communications can be applied to problems in businesses of many different types and sizes. The proliferation of computers and intelligent machines has created a need for some method to convey information throughout offices, between buildings, and to more distant locations quickly and reliably. Three different areas that could prosper from broadband networking are *the office of the future*, *the work-at-home concept*, and *small businesses*. Broadband technology provides the necessary resources and interfaces to meet the local, regional, and national requirements of these and other business communication applications.

Office of the Future

The aim of introducing advanced technology into the office workplace is to improve productivity. Productivity in offices has not kept pace with that of factories, where tremendous improvements have resulted from automation. Office automation is spreading in large and small companies; it includes the use of word processors, facsimile machines, intelligent copiers, computer terminals, and video conferencing equipment.

Broadband networking can provide an integrated solution to the problem of how to convey all the needed information to all the devices providing these services. Once the network is implemented, additional services can be added such as electronic mail, high-speed data transfer between workstations, integrated energy management, and access control.

Work-at-Home

The work-at-home concept has been popularized over the past several years. However, the high costs of implementing the required network and providing a home terminal slowed its growth. Terminal costs are predicted to soon be in the $250 range, making them cost effective for many users. Product announcements by major manufacturers indicate the cost of network implementation is also dropping rapidly.

Small Businesses

Networking in the small business sector could provide the impetus for the greatest integration of CATV and broadband local area networks. Thousands of companies throughout the United States could use individual broadband networks to supply their local requirements. These local networks could interface to CATV industrial trunks that supply communication links with other buildings (which could be several miles away).

The costs would be lower and the capabilities greater for a system using a broadband approach, compared to one using conventional wiring schemes for local networking.

The Industrial Community

The growth of factory automation has been tremendous over the past several years. This trend will continue as more intelligence is placed inside machines used directly on the factory floor, and as robots become commonplace in both large and small shops.

Current facilities have many distinct processors distributed throughout the plant. These are coupled into a loose network. Information passes between them as physical material, workpieces, and assemblies. Each machine must be programmed, and must provide various status signals back to the operator. A factory floor status reporting system can add further data on specific jobs and parts flow through the facility. Connecting all these devices together with a broadband network can provide the following advantages.

▶ More efficient use of machinery

▶ Improved scheduling of work and maintenance

▶ Better reporting of results

▶ Closer monitoring of machine performance

▶ Tighter control of factory performance and costs

A single broadband network can link a factory and an office to the automated data processing systems that support modern business operations. This integrated approach can provide timely information for all the following applications.

▶ Accounting

▶ Personnel management

▶ Time and attendance measurement

▶ Energy management

▶ Assembly line automation

▶ Program and schedule verification

In addition to providing a wide bandwidth medium that can be used by many different services, broadband coaxial cable is much less susceptible to electrical noise than twisted-pair wires. Both industrial and office environments contain radio frequency interference that could degrade the performance of a network and terminal equipment. It is best to assume the ambient levels of interference will become even greater, and to design networks protected to work properly under those conditions.

The Educational Community

Educational institutions are finding the broadband approach a reliable, economical, and efficient way to satisfy their communications requirements. These facilities have several unique needs that can be met by broadband networks.

▶ The wide geographical extent of a large campus can tax any communications system attempting to serve the whole area. Broadband networks have been successfully covering wide areas for years.

▶ Cost constraints demand a network that is low cost, easy to maintain, and vendor-independent. Broadband satisfies all three of these criteria.

Vendor independence means that the network offers a standard interface to which equipment from many different manufacturers can be attached.

1. The user is not limited to purchasing equipment from only one or a few vendors.

2. Many different types of equipment can be connected together over a single medium. The user can select terminals, workstations, and other devices from a wide range of available units, and choose those that provide the best cost and performance tradeoff for a specific application.

▶ Real-time video must be provided throughout the campus for closed-circuit television courses. Several one-way full bandwidth television channels can be reserved on the cable for this purpose.

▶ Other services could use the coaxial cable and minimize the installation and maintenance costs for communication services throughout the campus.

▶ Televised classes in the local community could be conveyed from the campus's broadband network to the city's local CATV network. A two-way path between these two networks could provide the campus with additional video signals from broadcasters and from other educational facilities.

Institutions including Brown, Cornell, Carnegie-Mellon, and the University of Waterloo have made extensive telecommunication studies, concluding that broadband distribution is a feasible and cost-effective approach to providing communication services.*

Network Examples

A fully activated broadband system (one with all return paths active) cannot be duplicated in a large CATV system covering a major city without special consideration. However, the industrial, educational, and business communities have seen few limitations to broadband local area network applications. As an example of possible broadband network size, a network in a West coast industrial plant covers an area greater than 3.6 million square feet of floor space on each of its two floors. Only 11 amplifiers support the entire network, which provides an RF connection within 100 feet of any point in the system.

Another system in the Chicago area provides 4000 RF outlets over six buildings, with no point farther than 20 feet from an outlet. This network also required only 11 amplifiers to support the six buildings, each of which has four floors of distribution.

A third example is a single system connecting six buildings. Within this complex, each building has from 9 to 23 floors of high-density outlet distribution (an outlet for each office). Only 21 amplifiers were required in this network. Also, a backup trunk was installed that can be switched into operation either automatically or manually if the primary circuit fails.

All three of these examples have operated successfully without a single amplifier module failure for a total of 12 system-years of operating experience. A broadband

---

* W.S. Shipp and H.H. Webber, "Final Report of the Study Group on Telecommunications and Networks," Brown University, Oct., 1980.

network can be counted on for continuous, daily operation. The high reliability of broadband components makes redundant backup devices necessary only for the most demanding networks.

If any of these networks had to expand to other facilities miles away, existing or new industrial trunks could be used. Such trunks could be installed and maintained by the local CATV company or by contractors working directly for the customer. In addition, microwave links, satellite links, and other services can provide the necessary resources for nationwide distribution of video or data.

Key Broadband Concepts

Introduction

This chapter introduces several important topics that will help in understanding broadband communication systems. Several of these areas are covered in more depth in the chapters indicated below.

- ▶ Topology
- ▶ Implementation (chapter three)
- ▶ Components (chapter four)
- ▶ Design issues (chapter five)

Network Topology

The arrangement of a broadband network is often described in two ways.

- ▶ Its *physical topology*: where the components are located.
- ▶ Its *logical topology* (*architecture*): how the components are connected to each other by the network.

Before discussing these two topologies, the main elements of a network must be defined. Every broadband network has two main elements, a headend and a distribution network.

- ▶ The *headend* comprises the equipment that collects RF signals from transmitting devices attached to the network, and distributes RF signals to receiving devices attached to the network. The term headend refers both to the location of this equipment, and to all the equipment that performs these functions.
- ▶ The *distribution network* comprises coaxial cables, amplifiers, and other signal-carrying components that provide signal paths between devices attached to the network and the headend.

Physical Topology

The placement of the headend and the distribution network determines the physical topology of the system. This topology can be portrayed by a map showing the location of these network elements. This map resembles a similar plot of other utility distribution systems (for example, telephone, electricity, water, or gas utilities), and can be compared to the structure of a tree.

1. It has a main trunk line that originates at the headend and traverses central areas.

2. It has many branch lines that extend from the trunk to outlying areas.

3. It has individual lines that run from each node on a branch to each connection point.

The trunk and branches form the *backbone network*. The backbone can usually support thousands of connections to user devices, with drop cables (connections to user outlets) installed as demand dictates (figure 2-1). In a large network, the headend is often located centrally so that the network can be extended easily in any direction.

The *nodes* of the network are determined by the location of the devices that use network services. Branch cables can be laid to connect the nodes in many different ways. Regardless of the layout chosen, each node connects to the cable system at only one point, and is independent of all other nodes. This structure eliminates any chance of multi-path distortion.

The physical layout of a broadband system can be designed to conform to any building arrangement. The flexibility of the broadband technique exceeds that of any other wiring scheme in use today.

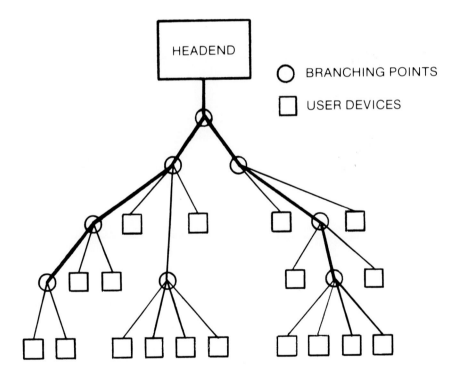

Figure 2-1. Inverted Tree Network Topology

The Headend

The headend is the origin of all RF signals transmitted to the entire network, and the destination of all RF signals generated by devices connected to the network.

▶ In a unidirectional CATV system, the headend transmits all the signals the network carries.

▶ In a bidirectional broadband system, both the headend and user devices transmit signals over the network.

Any device connected to the network may transmit signals over the network to other devices. However, these signals do not go directly to the destination device. Signals transmitted by devices connected to the network first go to the headend, and are then retransmitted back to the network. Routing all transmitted signals to the headend prevents interference among signals travelling on the system.

Equipment normally found in the headend of a large network that provides multiple services are signal processors, modulators, demodulators, signal combiners, data translation units, and power supplies. These devices are described in references dealing with CATV systems (see bibliography).

The Distribution Network

The distribution network is the combination of components that transfer RF signals between the headend and the attached user devices. These components include the following.

▶ Coaxial cables that carry signals between two points.

▶ Splitters, directional couplers, and taps that direct signal flow along desired paths.

▶ Filters that process signals depending on their frequency.

▶ Outlets that connect devices to the network.

▶ Amplifiers that increase signal strength.

Chapter four describes these components and their characteristics.

Logical Topology

From the local network point of view, the *logical topology* or *architecture* of the broadband network could be a ring, star, or bus. This level of organization is distinct from the physical topology, and depends on the LAN interface devices connected to the broadband network. A single broadband network can support several different types of local networks, each with a different logical topology.

In a bus network, all interface devices may have equal access to the network's resources. This structure requires a method to regulate transmissions and to prevent one device from monopolizing the network. Data communication networks have used such methods, called *channel access protocols*, for many years.

In a token-passing ring network, each interface device has permission to transmit when it receives a unique pattern of data over the network called the token. This station then transfers its data to the network and passes the token along, when finished, to the next station in the ring.

In a polled star network, a master controlling device grants permission to transmit to each connected station, one at a time. All communications traffic passes from the source device, to the central controller, and then to the destination device.

Other combinations of topologies and operating rules, or protocols, can be used on a broadband network. These communication protocols are provided by the interface devices attached to the network, and not by the backbone network itself. As long as interface devices can successfully get signals on and off the cable, they can send any kind of data using any kind of protocols.

Network Implementation: Single and Dual Cable Systems

Several different methods are available to provide two-way communication in a broadband network, including single and dual cable systems. *Single cable systems* carry two-way traffic on one coaxial cable. They provide this *bidirectional* capability by dividing the cable's frequency spectrum into two main portions, one for traffic in each direction. *Dual cable systems* use two separate coaxial cables, one for traffic in each direction.

When using a single cable to carry two-way traffic, the available signal spectrum on that cable is split into three major portions.

▶ The *forward band* carries signals from the headend to devices on the distribution network.

▶ The *return band* or *reverse band* carries signals from devices on the distribution network to the headend.

▶ The *guard band* carries no signals, and separates signals in the forward and return bands.

A dual cable system needs no guard band, since separate cables carry the *outbound* traffic (from the headend) and *inbound* traffic (to the headend).

Figure 2-2 illustrates frequency translation in a single cable system. Devices attached to the network transmit signals only in the return frequency band. All signals inside the return band are received at the headend and converted up to signals with higher frequencies by a device called a *translator*. These higher frequency signals, which occupy the forward band, are then transmitted to all receivers on the network.

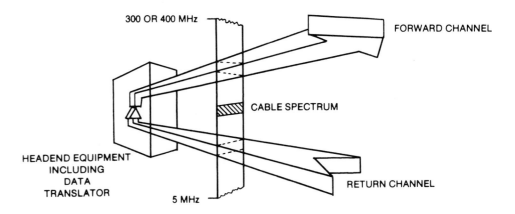

Figure 2-2. Bidirectional Communication: Frequency Translation

To visualize this concept, compare the broadband cable to a multilane highway. A highway has lanes going in both directions. The center divider (guard band) minimizes interference between the two directions and provides a boundary. A single cable supports two-way traffic exactly like a highway. A guard band of several megahertz separates the forward and return bands.

A highway has several lanes in each direction. A broadband cable has several channels for traffic in each direction.

Many different types of vehicles can use the general purpose highway lanes, including cars, trucks, motorcycles, and busses. Many different types of services can use the general purpose broadband channels on the network, including low- and high-speed data, voice, and video.

Some highway lanes can be reserved for specific uses only, such as busses or high-occupancy vehicles. Some channels on the cable system can be reserved for specific uses only. For example, one data communication channel might be reserved for users of a specific time-shared computer that can be accessed only via that channel.

The frequency spectrum of a single cable system can be divided in one of three ways. Each provides a different forward and return bandwidth (see table 2-1).

▶ The *subsplit format* is found on many older CATV systems. It has the least return path bandwidth of the three. It is usually the easiest format with which to upgrade an existing one-way system to two-way operation.

▶ The *midsplit format* provides more return path bandwidth than the subsplit; it is often used in contemporary broadband local area networks.

▶ The *highsplit format* is a recent innovation and will become more popular as more components become available for it. It provides the greatest return bandwidth of these three formats.

All three of these frequency divisions are further described in chapter three.

Table 2-1.
Bidirectional Single-Cable Systems

Format	Return Frequency Band	Forward Frequency Band
Subsplit	5-30 MHz	54-400 MHz
Midsplit	5-116 MHz	168-400 MHz
Highsplit	5-174 MHz	232-400 MHz

Figure 2-3 shows a simple single-cable network layout including the headend translator and the distribution network. The arrows show the direction of signal flow from the transmitting unit, through the headend translator, to the intended receiving unit. Full duplex operation is possible because different frequencies are used for transmitting and receiving.

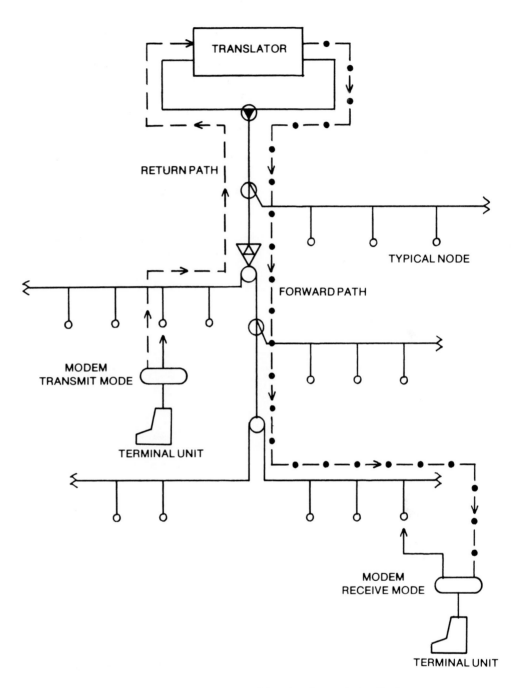

Figure 2-3. Bidirectional Communication: Full Duplex Transmission Paths

Components

The components used in a broadband network can be divided into two categories, active and passive. *Active* components require input power to operate properly; *passive* components do not. Chapter four discusses components in more detail.

The most ubiquitous component in a broadband network is coaxial cable. It is the transmission medium for all signals on the network. A coaxial cable is constructed of a solid center conductor surrounded by a uniform thickness of insulating or dielectric material. These are thoroughly covered by a second layer of conducting material (the *shield*) and the final exterior insulation. Both conductors have a common axis, hence the name coaxial.

Conductor resistance and dielectric conductance are distributed uniformly along the length of the cable, and vary with frequency and temperature. Because of these variations, the frequency response of coaxial cable varies with the following parameters.

▶ Length and diameter of the cable

▶ Frequency of the signal

▶ Ambient temperature

These variations must be considered when designing and installing a system.

Some of the significant characteristics and capabilities of coaxial cable include the following.

▶ High bandwidth.

Coaxial cables can convey wider bandwidth signals than twisted pair wiring. Cable bandwidth exceeds that of active and passive RF network components.

▶ Shielding.

When properly grounded, the cable's shield (outer conductor) prevents ambient electrical noise from interfering with signals travelling on the center conductor. Thus, coaxial cable is a good transmission medium for use in electrically noisy environments (including offices, laboratories, and factories).

▶ Easy connectivity.

A cable can be quickly and easily cut and spliced to repair a break or to attach new outlets, devices, or cable paths.

▶ Characteristic impedance.

Most cables used in broadband systems have a 75-ohm characteristic impedance.

▶ Diameter.

Larger diameter cables have less loss than smaller diameter cables and are therefore used for main trunks and for long cable runs.
Smaller cables have more loss, but are more flexible and easier to manipulate and install. Branch cables and drop cables (connecting network devices to the system) are usually smaller than trunk cables.

▶ Power.

Cables with seamless aluminum shielding can safely transport ac or dc power to amplifiers on the network. By sending power over the cable, each amplifier does not need a separate connection to a power source.

▶ Wide selection.

Coaxial cables have been made for several decades by many manufacturers. The technology is well known and the product is reliable. Cables with appropriate characteristics are available for rough environments and other special applications.

Cable attenuation is commonly specified in decibels per 100 feet at the highest operating frequency (300 or 400 MHz for most systems). A typical cable specification provided by the manufacturer could be stated in the following manner.

1.63 dB of loss per 100 feet at 300 MHz measured at 68 degrees Fahrenheit.

This represents the specification of one type of 0.412-inch diameter seamless aluminum coaxial cable.

To calculate the signal loss of a 1000-foot length of this cable, simply multiply 1.63 by 10 which gives 16.3 dB. By using the attenuation factors for each frequency band, the loss of any given length of cable for those bands can be calculated.

Following chapters contain more information on coaxial cables. Chapter four provides further details on their characteristics. Chapter five discusses cable selection.

Design Issues

This section introduces three concepts related to signal levels that are important to the design of broadband networks.

▶ Using decibels to indicate signal levels simplifies all network signal level calculations.

▶ The unity gain criterion eases system design and alignment.

▶ Transparent system design ensures geographical independence of the network.

This discussion points out some of the advantages of properly designed broadband networks. Further coverage of backbone network design is provided in chapter five.

Achieving Proper Signal Levels

Once the basic topology is determined, the distribution network can be designed to supply proper signal levels to each connection. The design engineer selects the components that meet the system's physical and electrical specifications, and calculates the signal loss along each path. Where computations indicate signal levels will be too low, amplifiers can be inserted to increase them. The calculations are then repeated for every path that each new amplifier affects, and other components might have to be changed to achieve specified signal levels. This process is repeated until all signal levels are within specified ranges.

As an analogy to RF signal distribution, consider a simple water delivery system. The purpose is to provide a specified water pressure to three destinations, which might be done in the following manner.

1. Build a large main delivery line from the reservoir to each location.

2. Install valves at each location.

3. Adjust each valve to deliver the required water pressure. If the pressure is too low, either add pumps or increase the pressure in the main delivery line.

The basic principles of RF design are similar. The main RF trunk cable corresponds to the main delivery line. Passive taps and couplers act like valves that determine the signal level at each outlet. Amplifiers increase signal strength where it is too low.

Signal Amplitude: the Decibel (dB)

Calculating signal levels throughout an entire system can be time-consuming, especially when several channels and amplifiers are involved. This task is made easier by expressing signal levels in logarithmic units.

The *decibel* is a unit that expresses the ratio of two levels of power. It can also be used to express the ratio of two voltage or current values, if they are measured at points of similar impedance. For example, many network components have an input and an output connection. The ratio of the signal levels at these two points can be expressed in decibels, such as an attenuator with 3 dB of loss, or an amplifier with 20 dB of gain, from input to output.

Number of dB $= 10\log (P_1/P_2)$	
$= 20\log (V_1/V_2)$	
where	P_1, P_2 are power levels
	V_1, V_2 are voltage levels
	log is the base ten logarithm

A standard unit used in the CATV industry to express signal amplitude is the *decibel referred to one millivolt (dBmV)*.

Number of dBmV $= 20\log (V_1/1\text{mV})$	
where	$V_1 =$ the measured voltage level
	$0 \text{ dBmV} = 1 \text{ mV} = 1000 \ \mu V$ across a 75-ohm load

Using absolute voltage levels instead of decibels to calculate signal levels requires calculations that become more complex as more components and channels are added to a system. Using dBmV to calculate signal levels allows easier manipulation of those values. The gain or loss, in decibels, of a component is added to or subtracted from its input signal level to obtain its output signal level. Also, fractional values can be avoided, since any number between zero and one is represented by a negative number of decibels. For example,

▶ A 40-dB amplifier increases its input signal voltage level by 100 times;

▶ A 6-dB coupler decreases its input signal level by one-half;

▶ A video signal level of 10 dBmV for a specific channel at any given outlet is 3,200 μV.

Because decibels are easy to use, all relevant equipment specifications and signal requirements are expressed in dBmV or dB. The difference between two dBmV values is expressed in dB. For example, a typical carrier-to-noise ratio is 43 dB and can be obtained by subtracting the measured noise floor (in dBmV) from the input signal level of an amplifier (in dBmV). Both the input level and the noise floor are expressed in dBmV, but the mathematical result is expressed in dB. Thus, dB is a ratio while dBmV is an expression of signal amplitude.

Table 2-2 provides a short conversion chart for translating between dBmV and voltage. Appendix L contains a more detailed table. Note that all levels below 1000μV (0 dBmV) are negative values.

Table 2-2.
dBmV/Volt Conversion Chart

dBmV	Voltage
80	10.0 Volts
70	3.2
60	1.0
50	320,000 μV
40	100,000
30	32,000
20	10,000
10	3,200
0	1,000
−10	320
−20	100
−30	32
−40	10

Unity Gain Trunk Design

When designing the trunk portion of the distribution system, the unity gain criterion should be followed.

Unity Gain Criterion

1. All trunk amplifiers are identical (with respect to noise figure, gain and equalization).

2. All trunk amplifiers are separated by an identical length of cable.

3. Flat Loss + Cable Loss = Amplifier Gain.

Result: All trunk amplifier output levels are identical.

Designing the trunk to this standard provides these advantages.

▶   The system is easy to design by consistently following this rule.

▶   The system is easy to align and maintain, since the output levels of all amplifiers are identical.

This rule requires that either each trunk amplifier be adjusted to compensate for the losses between its input point and the previous amplifier's output point (see figure 2-4); or that each trunk amplifier be adjusted to compensate for the losses between its output point and the following amplifier's input point. Thus each amplifier in the system has the same output signal level, and the system has unity gain throughout (no increase or decrease in signal level from one amplifier's output to the next).

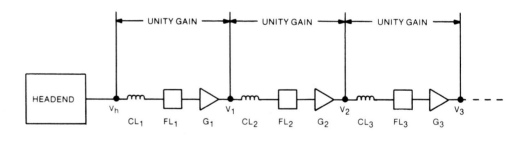

CL = CABLE LOSS (dB)
FL = FLAT LOSS (dB)
G = AMPLIFIER GAIN (dB)
V = SIGNAL VOLTAGE LEVEL (dBmV)

$V_h = V_1 = V_2 = V_3$

$G_n = CL_n + FL_n$

Figure 2-4. Unity Gain in a System

System Losses

The distribution system's losses can be divided into two main categories, flat loss and cable loss.

▶ *Flat loss*, or *passive loss*, is the attenuation through all the passive components in the network (not including the cable). The value of this loss is constant across the entire frequency spectrum.

▶ *Cable loss* is the attenuation of the coaxial cable. This loss increases with frequency, a characteristic called *cable tilt*.

To achieve the same amplitude for all signals at all frequencies of interest, it is necessary to compensate for both flat loss and cable loss. This is accomplished with equalizers and amplifiers.

An *equalizer* has an attenuation characteristic that is the inverse of the cable tilt with respect to frequency. It attenuates low frequency signals more than high frequency signals. Ideally, the combined cable and equalizer losses produce constant attenuation across the system's entire bandwidth.

A flat gain amplifier following the equalizer increases signal levels across the spectrum. Figure 2-5 demonstrates unity gain and shows how one stage of a network compensates for cable tilt.

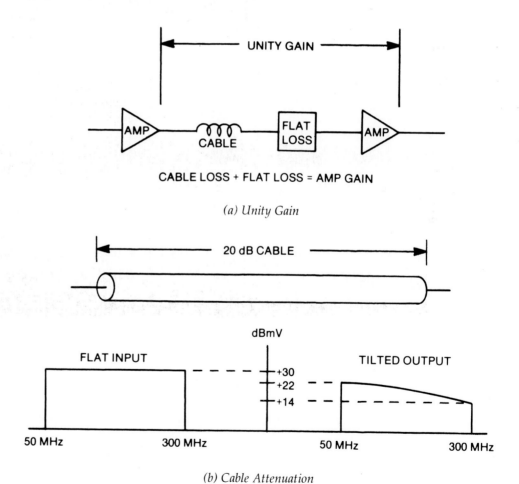

(a) Unity Gain

(b) Cable Attenuation

Figure 2-5. Unity Gain of One Stage

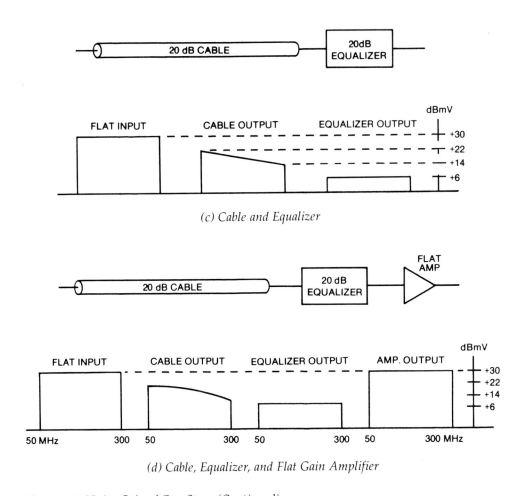

(c) Cable and Equalizer

(d) Cable, Equalizer, and Flat Gain Amplifier

Figure 2-5. Unity Gain of One Stage (Continued)

Transparent System Design

During the design phase, a standard signal level should be established for all outlets in a system. When this is done, connectivity requirements for the network are *transparent*. Any device can be attached to any outlet and use the same network services, regardless of its location and function. The input and output circuits of a network interface device need be adjusted only once for the standard system levels, after which the device can be used anywhere in the network. Thus, transparency provides the following advantages.

▶ Easy relocation of devices throughout the network.
▶ Easy connection of new devices to the network.

For example, a network interface device can be moved from one office to another, and plugged into the second office's outlet. At the new location, it can use and provide the same services that it did at the old location. If the network was not transparent, signal level differences at the two outlets might require adjustment of the interface device whenever it was moved.

Many devices designed to communicate over broadband networks are built to receive at a level of +6 dBmV, and to transmit at a level of +56 dBmV (referred to a television visual carrier signal in a 6 MHz channel). By designing the network to accommodate these signal levels, any such device could be used at any outlet without requiring installation adjustments. (Signal levels are covered in more detail in chapter five.)

Summary

This chapter covered several essential topics in broadband networking. The physical structure of the network resembles a tree. Attached communication devices see it as a bus, a ring, or a star. Channel protocols are used to control access to channels that have more than a single transmitter on them.

Two-way communication can be accomplished with two one-way cables, or with a single two-way cable that has a separate frequency band for traffic in each direction.

The transmission medium for broadband networks is coaxial cable. Many different types of coaxial cables are available that have characteristics to match various applications.

Network design calculations are facilitated by using decibels instead of Volts and Watts. Signal levels established at the design phase should permit easy alignment and maintenance. Following the unity gain principle, and designing for transparent connectivity eases both of these tasks.

Single and Dual Cable Systems

Introduction

To achieve bidirectional signal distribution, two basic approaches can be employed.

▶ Two-way communications over a single coaxial cable, with different frequency bands carrying signals in opposite directions.

▶ Two-way communications over dual coaxial cables, with each cable carrying signals in one direction.

This chapter discusses both approaches, shows how they can be be used together, and compares their capabilities.

Single Cable Systems

Two-way communications can be implemented on a single coaxial cable by dividing the available frequency spectrum on the cable into two bands. These bands carry signals in opposite directions, called *forward* (away from the headend) and *return* or *reverse* (toward the headend). Devices attached to the network transmit to the headend on the return band, and receive from the headend on the forward band. Currently, three different frequency divisions are used, called subsplit, midsplit, and highsplit. Each provides a different amount of forward and return bandwidth.

When specifying CATV equipment for a network, be aware that manufacturers use slightly different frequencies and bandwidths. Check each component's specifications to ensure that all equipment in the system is compatible, and that any filters can pass all the signals being transported.

Subsplit System

Most CATV two-way cable systems now in service use the subsplit format.

▶ Forward band 54-400 MHz

▶ Reverse band 5-30 MHz

▶ Total usable bandwidth 371 MHz

This system has been popular with CATV system operators because it offers the easiest method to upgrade existing one-way cable systems to two-way operation. It allows transmission of all 12 VHF television channels on their normal broadcast frequency assignments, which eliminates the need for special converters at each customer's site.

However, when more than 12 channels are to be distributed over a single cable system, separate converters are necessary anyway, eliminating this advantage for many systems.

The subsplit format has limited utility when information originates from locations other than the headend. Since only 25 MHz is available in the return direction, only four television signals or their bandwidth equivalent can be transported to the headend at one time. The impact of this limitation depends on the type of equipment used in the network. Microprocessor-based packet communication units available today permit data networks with thousands of users to operate on a single 6-MHz channel.

Midsplit System

Midsplit systems are used in many data communication networks.

▶ Forward band 168 to 400 MHz

▶ Reverse band 5 to 116 MHz

▶ Total usable bandwidth 343 MHz

Midsplit is more popular than subsplit for local area networks, because of its greater return direction bandwidth. It can handle high volume two-way interactive communications including data (both low- and high-speed) and video. The IEEE-802 specification (a standard currently being developed for local area networks) for such networks endorses this format.

A midsplit system's greater bandwidth can be used by one or more services. For example, when using a modem with a bandwidth efficiency of 2 bits per Hertz, a T1 channel (which conveys digital data at 1.544 Mbits/s) occupies only 772 kHz. A midsplit system can provide over 140 such channels in its return path.

Figure 3-1 shows block diagrams of trunk amplifiers for subsplit and midsplit systems. Appendix C summarizes the symbols used in this and other drawings in the book.

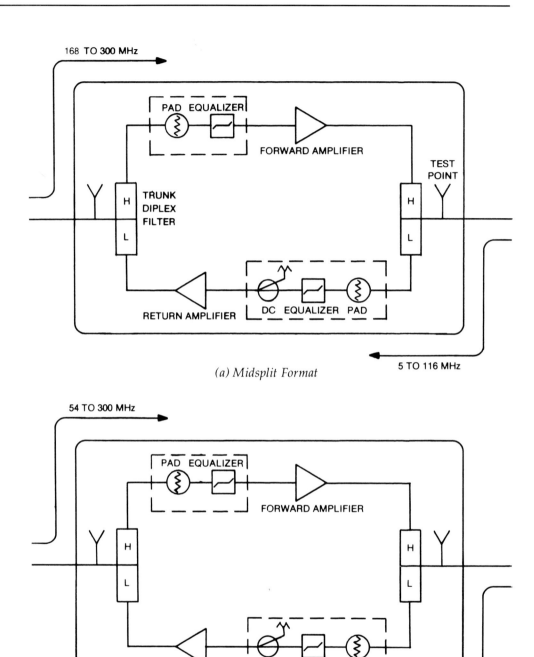

(a) Midsplit Format

(b) Subsplit Format

Figure 3-1. Typical Two-Way Cable Trunk Amplifiers

Highsplit System

This is the newest system of the three.

▶ Forward band 232-400 MHz
▶ Reverse band 5-174 MHz
▶ Total usable bandwidth 337 MHz

A highsplit system fulfills the need for high return path bandwidth that some large systems might have. Some amplifiers are now available in the highsplit format, but standardization among vendors of these units has not yet been achieved.

Converting From A One-Way To A Two-Way System

The following factors should be considered when converting an existing one-way network into a two-way midsplit network.

▶ Use of individual frequency converters at each user device.
▶ Expandability of present amplifiers to bidirectional use.
▶ Redefinition of system frequency allocations.
▶ Modification of existing services and their frequency allocations.
▶ Selection of passive components that pass all the required frequencies.
▶ Inspection of existing coaxial cables. Inspect them to ensure signal ingress will not cause problems.

It is not necessary to disrupt service while upgrading a system to support two-way traffic. Modular amplifier units allow easy installation of return amplifiers, equalizers, and distribution legs in the field.

One study from the cable industry estimates that existing one-way networks can be upgraded to two-way subsplit networks at a cost of around $300 per mile.*

Dual Cable Systems

Two-way dual cable systems use two coaxial cables laid side-by-side. One cable provides the inbound (return) path signals to the headend. The second cable provides the outbound (forward) path signals from the headend to the attached devices.

▶ Outbound band 40-400 MHz
▶ Inbound band 40-400 MHz
▶ Total usable bandwidth 360 MHz

Not all dual cable networks use this same spectrum. For example, Wang Laboratories' network uses non-standard amplifiers with a bandpass of 10 to 350 MHz.

---

* Ellis Simon, "Cable's Business Connection," Cable Marketing Magazine, January, 1982.

Each outlet in a dual cable system must have two connections that clearly identify the inbound and outbound paths. In addition, twice as many amplifier units are required to implement a dual cable network, compared to a single cable network.

The term *amplifier unit* refers to the module that contains the gain block, power supply, equalizers, and any associated circuitry. Currently one vendor supplies all the necessary circuitry for both paths of a dual cable system inside a single module. Shielding and isolation requirements dictated against placing circuitry for both directions inside the same enclosure for many years, until improved isolation methods were perfected.

Dual cable system amplifiers are used in the unidirectional mode with a bandpass of 54 to 400 MHz. Figure 3-2 shows the block diagram of a dual cable amplifier.

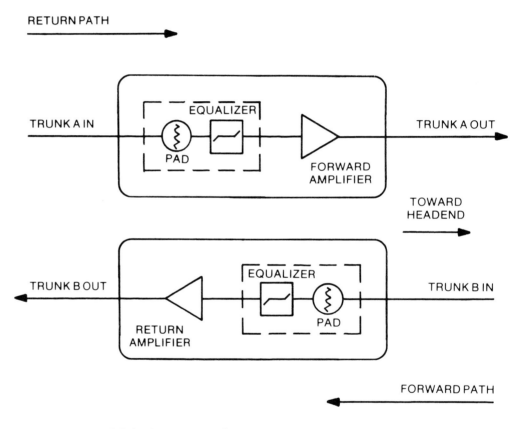

Figure 3-2. *Dual Cable System Amplifier*

Dual cable systems have no interaction between inbound and outbound signals except when devices are incorrectly connected to the network. No special filters are required in amplifiers to provide frequency separation. As a result, amplitude and phase distortion in a dual cable network are less than in a single cable network.

CATV Dual Trunk Systems

The two-way dual cable systems described in the preceding section are not the same as CATV dual trunk systems. *CATV dual trunk systems* are composed of two one-way trunks laid side-by-side to each subscriber's location. The subscriber selects signals from only one trunk at a time with an A/B switch. This technique was a simple way for early CATV systems to double their signal bandwidth. The A/B switch directs the signals from one trunk to the television receiver and isolates the signals on the other trunk from the receiver. Some CATV operators have converted one of these trunks into a two-way system. When the proper trunk is selected by the user, two-way operation is possible.

Connecting Networks Together

Separate networks connect to a common trunk through devices called *gateways* (see figure 3-3). These devices can be set to pass only a selected frequency band so that each user can be isolated from other users on the common trunk. One well-known system currently using this approach is in the New York area. Manhattan Cable Television provides a dedicated commercial trunk to serve the banking community in New York's financial district. This trunk is primarily used for passing data from one branch of a bank to another. Other gateways can connect to national data transmission networks

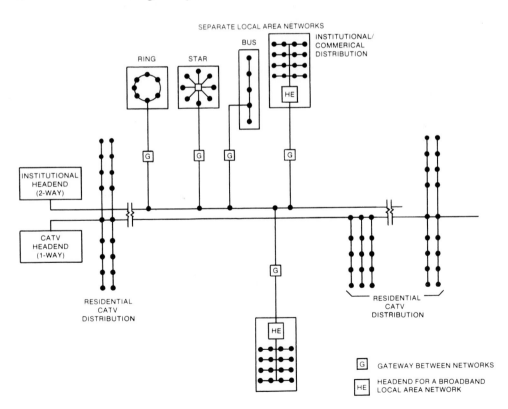

Figure 3-3. Interconnecting LANs with Industrial Trunking

such as TeleNet and Tymnet and extend the range of a local area network across the country. This technique (called *industrial trunking*) is primarily used in CATV systems to provide dedicated or shared networks for industrial and business users.

Current technology does not permit two-way transmission over the full extent of a large CATV network. However, one or more portions of a large network can be made bidirectional to provide wideband communication links between nearby sites, such as individual local area networks. A device on one local network needing to access a device on another local network can do so over the CATV trunk (figure 3-3).

Single and dual cable systems can be combined together into useful network structures. Figure 3-4 illustrates samples of these combinations. At first glance the structures might appear complicated. However, they are simply expansions or reconfigurations of basic single and dual cable structures.

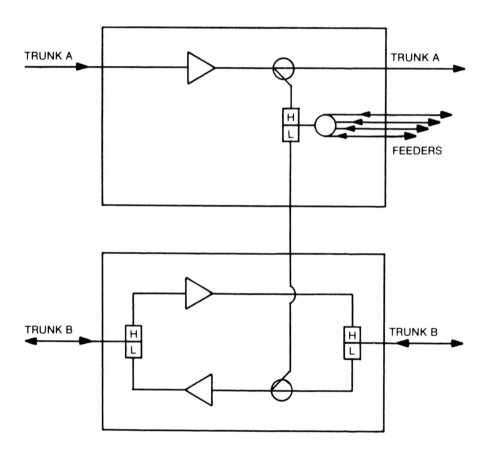

(a) Dual Trunk/Single Feeder

Figure 3-4. Combined Single and Dual Cable Systems

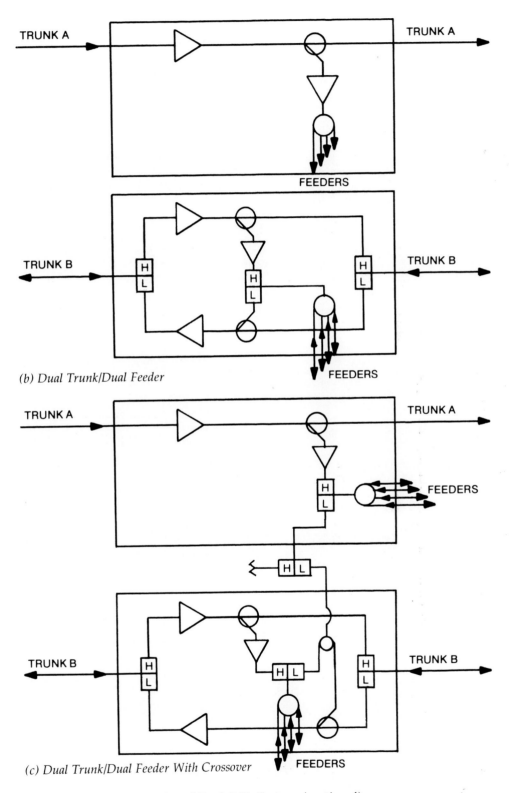

(b) Dual Trunk/Dual Feeder

(c) Dual Trunk/Dual Feeder With Crossover

Figure 3-4. Combined Single and Dual Cable Systems (continued)

Comparing Single and Dual Cable Systems

This section discusses several advantages and disadvantages of single and dual cable systems to assist in determining where one approach is more suitable than the other.

System Bandwidth

Although it is difficult to generalize for all networks, 60 MHz of bandwidth in each direction has proven adequate for many applications. Several systems use only about 35% of the total bandwidth available.

Where wide bandwidth is necessary, there are two alternatives.

▶ A dual cable system can be implemented.

▶ Two separate single cable systems, each carrying different services, can be implemented side-by-side.

Two single cable systems provide all the advantages of the single cable method including simpler design, maintenance, and installation, in addition to increased bandwidth and system redundancy. The disadvantages of this approach are cable identification, trunk switching, and more complicated documentation requirements.

When applications require more than about 100 MHz in the return path, it is more cost effective to install two midsplit cables instead of one dual cable system. This provides 222 MHz in the return path and 464 MHz in the forward path.

Multiple Cable Systems

One alternative to a large cable system throughout a facility is to build several distinct and complete systems that serve various subdivisions of that facility. At first glance, this scheme might seem to offer several advantages over either a dual cable or two single cables where large bandwidth is required in the entire facility. However, it has some serious drawbacks.

▶ Confusing layout

▶ Redundant cabling and equipment

▶ Duplication of resources

▶ Diffused responsibility for maintenance

A better solution is to have an intra-plant cable trunk that provides the backbone for shared services throughout the entire complex. Connected to this trunk are branches that feed each building. Inside each building, one cable network provides the necessary services. This approach is simpler to design, easier to maintain, and allows better management of system noise.

Amplifier Capacity

One disadvantage of using high-bandwidth systems is that the capacity of the amplifiers might not be great enough to handle the maximum load. For example, assume that one 6-MHz channel contains 56 separate data carriers that use subchannels of 96 kHz bandwidth each. If each carrier is transmitted at a level of $+56$ dBmV, the amplifiers are loaded with the equivalent of 56 separate 6 MHz-wide channels at a $+56$ dBmV signal level. All the power capacity of the amplifiers could be consumed by the signals from only 6 MHz of the spectrum, preventing any other signals from being transmitted. In addition, this would distort each amplifier's output signal excessively, and interfering signals could be generated at harmonic frequencies throughout the spectrum.

To prevent overloading the amplifiers, narrow bandwidth data signals should be transmitted at lower levels than wide bandwidth video signals. The amount of this signal level difference depends on the number of carrier signals inside a 6-MHz channel. Chapter five contains examples showing how to calculate what is called the *derated carrier level* for this situation. These calculations are straightforward, since single cable networks using the same CATV technology and components have been successfully applied for several years. CATV amplifiers are capable of full channel loading, and the proper operating levels are well known in the industry.

Amplifier loading and data carrier derating can be a problem in dual cable systems where the amplifiers must pass a much wider bandwidth. The proper operating levels for such wideband networks have not been clearly established yet.

Components

Amplifiers for dual cable systems cost less than those for single cable systems. This is because each dual cable amplifier housing does not hold the extra components (filters and a second amplifier) used by the single cable system. However, twice as many amplifier housings can be required in a dual cable system. Two separate housings are commonly used in most systems.

Most amplifiers for single cable systems operate in standard frequency ranges and with standard bandpasses. Subsplit and midsplit amplifiers are available from many vendors. However, some dual cable systems use different frequencies and bandwidths than others. Amplifiers for such systems might not be available from several sources, which could lead to supply and repair problems.

Dual cable systems do not require the translator that single cable systems need.

Interface equipment for dual cable systems must keep signals from the two paths isolated from each other while extracting the data from the RF carriers. Circuits that achieve the necessary isolation can add to the cost of the interface device.

Installation

Dual cable systems take up more space than single cable systems because they use twice as much cable, and they need twice as many amplifiers, passive components, and other hardware. When retrofitting an existing facility, mounting space can be critical and the smaller requirements of the single cable system are an advantage.

In addition, single cable systems are easier to install because all the directional components face the same way. In a dual cable network, these components must be placed in different directions, depending on the cable to which they attach.

Maintenance

Repairing both single and dual cable systems is easier if the network has been designed and built with proper components. Maintaining and troubleshooting the single cable network is easier because of its simpler implementation with fewer cables and components. It is easier to follow drawings and trace cables through the single cable plant because there are no directional markings that could be incorrect.

The abundance of cables at every branching point can be confusing when trying to trace the loop from source to destination in a dual cable system. Each piece of cable must be marked correctly throughout the network to minimize the chance of mistakes during connection.

Single cable systems also offer better reliability since they use fewer components.

Interface to Other Networks

Most industrial and institutional trunks provided by the CATV industry are single cable systems. An in-house single cable system can be connected to such trunks more easily than can a dual cable system. It can be desirable to use such services, since bandwidth rental costs average from 10% to 20% lower than equivalent services from the local telephone company.

Redundancy

The purpose of redundancy is to provide a backup for important network services when the primary network is damaged. Single cable networks can provide redundancy by installing a second cable system throughout the facility. A breakdown on one cable leaves a functional system albeit with lower performance. On the other hand, losing one cable of a dual cable system would eliminate traffic in one direction entirely, making two-way communication impossible.

Running two single cable systems side-by-side lowers the cost of installing the second network. However, two cables along the same path do not provide as much protection against failure as two totally different paths would. Alignment of both routes of the system is straightforward, and tracing problems is only slightly more difficult. Each outlet would have two connectors that could provide identical services.

A redundant dual cable network requires twice the cable, amplifiers, hardware, and other components of a redundant single cable network. There are four cables in the system for each drop and four separate connectors at each outlet. Each of four cables at every location must be identified clearly.

▶ The primary inbound
▶ The primary outbound
▶ The backup inbound
▶ The backup outbound

Trying to trace a signal in a ceiling at a four-way splitter could be cumbersome. This maze of cables is exactly what local area networking is intended to eliminate.

Outlets

Since the outlet is the one component that the user sees and might have to manipulate, it should have a clear and simple design. Many different types of single cable outlets are available, including self-terminating devices. These provide protection from signal ingress and egress and maintain proper matching in the network. They can also meet military and government requirements for network security. The use of standard RF connectors enables repairs to be made quickly, using inexpensive tools.

Dual cable outlets require two separate connectors at each outlet. To prevent installers and users from crossing the paths at the outlet, two different types of connectors are recommended. When a second, redundant path is required, four connectors must be installed at each outlet. If the installation uses nonstandard RF connectors, maintenance problems could arise. When a connector breaks, Murphy's law will prevail and there will be every type of connector on hand except the one that is needed.

Future Developments

The development of cable communications over the past years has dictated some changes in user equipment and system choices. When precise wideband equipment was not available, the only way to obtain additional signal bandwidth was to use a second coaxial cable. As better components and techniques were employed in the design of RF data modems, more signals could be placed in narrower frequency bands. Also, many more users could be connected to a network without degrading its response. These factors enable more users to operate on less cable spectrum than in the past. This means that a modern single cable system can provide more capacity at a lower cost than an older dual cable system.

Most current broadband local area networks use only seven channels (42 MHz) or less for video conferencing and video security applications. Increased bandwidth will be necessary as new video applications requiring interactive control arise, such as the following.

▶ Videotext servers that provide individually addressable video frames.

▶ Video switchers that route signals throughout a network.

▶ Remote-controlled video tape recorders and video disk players that can be used interactively for teaching and entertainment.

By expanding a single cable network from 300 to 400 MHz, 16 additional 6-MHz channels are available for such services. Upgrading a network in this way can be more economical than either installing a second cable or installing a dual cable network originally. Advances in bandwidth compression could bring such services to single cable networks without requiring extensive modification.

Conclusions

Several studies have concluded that the single cable system is the best method with which to implement broadband local area networks. Cox Cable Communications found that both one-way and interactive two-way services can best be provided by a packetized data service on a single cable network. Other Multiple Station Operators (MSOs) have tested frequency agile modems in networks with over 20 amplifiers in forward cascade. The results have been data bit error rates from a worst case of one in 10^8 to one in 10^9 bits transmitted, with a noise level between 15 and 27 dB below peak video carrier on the system. A one-way network upgraded to two-way operation can supply a much better 44 dB carrier-to-noise ratio for the return path with about 200 miles of cable plant activated.*

In general, technology, cost, and installation considerations favor the use of single cable systems for the distribution of RF signals for data processing, audio, video, and control applications. However, each application should be analyzed critically with all the above points in mind before choosing between a single or dual cable system.

---

* Claude Baggett, Paul Workman, Michael Ellis, "Upstream Noise and Bit-Error Rates Analysis of an Operational One-Way System Converted to Two-Way Operation," *Cable '81 Technical Papers: The Future of Communications*, ed., NCTA (1981).

Broadband Components

Introduction

This chapter describes various broadband system components. All passive and active components discussed have 75 ohms impedance and provide 100 dB or better shielding from radio frequency interference (RFI), electromagnetic interference (EMI), and signal ingress. Appendix G lists some of the tools needed to install and maintain these components.

The Coaxial Cable

Chapter 2 described coaxial cable and briefly mentioned some of its features. This section provides a more detailed examination of some specific properties and uses of coaxial cable for broadband networks. The types of cable used in broadband networks can be divided into three application categories: trunks, feeders, and drops. These can be installed with or without conduits, depending on the insulation material, the environment, and local building codes. Finally, the variations of cable attenuation with frequency and temperature are covered.

Because it has been useful in so many applications, coaxial cable has developed greatly over the past decades. Even the least expensive cable can provide 80 dB shielding effectiveness and low loss across a 400 MHz bandwidth. Figure 4-1 shows the composition of a typical coaxial trunk cable.

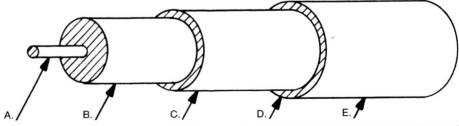

A.   CENTER CONDUCTOR: Centermost feature of coaxial cable, it consists of solid cooper or copper clad aluminum wire.

B.   DIELECTRIC: Electrical insulation utilized to maintain position of the center conductor. It is composed of foamed polyethylene. This insulator/positioner may also be evenly spaced polyethylene discs.

C.   OUTER CONDUCTOR: Is constructed of an aluminum tube. The cable size (412, 500, 750 & 1000) is derived from its outside diameter.

D.   FLOODING COMPOUND: (OPTIONAL) A viscous substance placed between the outer conductor C and the jacket E to maintain a protective seal should the jacket E contain or develop any cuts or openings.

E.   JACKET: (OPTIONAL) A black polyethylene coating over the aluminum outer conductor to provide a weather-tight seal.

Figure 4-1. Terminology for Coaxial Trunk Cable

Types of Cables

Cables used in coaxial cable networks can be divided into three layers.

▶ The first layer, the *trunk cable*, transports signals between amplifiers.
▶ The second layer, the *distribution* or *feeder cable*, connects the trunk cable to the vicinity of the subscriber or office.
▶ The third layer, the *drop cable*, links the feeder cable to the outlet.

Trunk Cables

Trunk lines come in six sizes, ranging from 0.412 to 1.000 inches in diameter. These cables exhibit attenuations from 1.6 to 0.5 dB per 100 feet (at 300 MHz). Their construction includes a rigid aluminum shield of seamless tubing with a bending radius of 10 times the diameter, covered with a strong polyethylene jacket. In some cables, a flooding compound is injected between the aluminum shield and the outer jacket to provide protection in underground installations. Inside the shield a foam dielectric surrounds the solid copper or copper clad aluminum center conductor.

Generally, all trunk lines should be 0.500 inches or larger in diameter. Cables run outside buildings or mounted to poles are usually jacketed. Cables buried or placed in conduits should use corrosion-resistant flooding gel between the outer jacket and the aluminum shield. The gel protects the aluminum from corrosion if the jacket is cut or damaged. Armored cable with flooding gel is mandatory where the cable is buried underground without further protection, and where it is mounted in underground vaults and might be damaged by water or rodents.

Cables with messengers are available for suspension between buildings or on poles. This feature provides protection and eliminates the need for strand lines.

Feeder Cables

Smaller-sized trunk cables are used for feeder cables. These indoor cables are selected according to the following criteria.

▶ The physical constraints of the building: smaller cables are easier to install.
▶ The required signal level for the distribution network: larger cables have less signal loss.
▶ Local and national building codes.

In general, jacketed or unjacketed 0.500-inch aluminum cables are used for trunks and feeders.

Drop Cables

Drop cables connect feeder cables to network outlets. These cables need not be very large, since only one cable is used for each outlet. They range from RG-11 and RG-6 to RG-59. Each type incorporates foil and braid shielding to prevent radiation and pickup of RF energy. The outer jacket is made of an insulating material.

Drop cable lengths vary from 10 to 50 feet. They can be installed above ceilings and through walls. A drop can connect directly to a wall outlet or to a device such as a television receiver, modulator, demodulator, or data modem. To minimize pickup of noise and broadcasted RF signals, the best quality and best shielded cable should be used for drops.

Installation Considerations

Cables can be installed throughout a facility with or without conduits. This choice depends on the type of insulation used by the cable, and on building codes. Fire codes might prohibit PVC-coated cables in ceiling plenums or computer floors because toxic fumes could be circulated if a fire occurred. In these cases, PVC cable can be placed inside a conduit, or cable with a fire-retardant jacket (such as Teflon™) can be used.

To compare the cost of using Teflon-insulated cables to installing conduit, consider the following approximate data.

▶ *Teflon cable.*

The cost per 1000 feet of Teflon cable is higher than that of PVC cable (1984 price quotes range from $0.50 to $1.50 per foot).

Installation of Teflon cable is more expensive than PVC cable because of special connectors and longer labor time to install these connectors.

▶ *Conduit.*

A *rule-of-thumb* states conduit installation cost, including materials, to be around $1 per foot.

Conduit provides additional physical protection for the cable, and additional shielding from radiated signals.

During construction, buildings can be piped with conduit for cables. Passive components and amplifiers should be installed inside enclosures appropriate for the environment. Each enclosure should be located to provide access for alignment and maintenance.

Proper ventilation should be provided for components mounted inside enclosures. It is important to maintain the temperature inside the amplifier housing as close as possible to the temperature experienced by the cable. Enclosures installed inside buildings might require fans to prevent heat build-up. Enclosures installed outdoors might not need fans, depending on the amplifier's operating temperature range and environmental conditions.

Although coaxial cable is durable, it is not invulnerable. When transporting and installing coaxial cables, always handle them carefully. The cable should be left uncut and fastened securely until it is required for installation. During installation the cable should not be kinked or bent beyond the specified limits.

In overhead installations, several factors relating to safely mounting coaxial cables must be considered. A good source of information is the article "Guidelines for Handling Trunk and Feeder Cables"* from Times Fiber Communications. This article is easy to read and highly informative on cable-handling techniques including tension factors, cable reels, and pulling limitations.

Teflon™ is a registered trademark of DuPont.

* Coaxial Cable Catalog, Times Fiber Communications, January, 1982.

Cable Attenuation

The attenuation of a coaxial cable is often quoted as a single number, such as 10 dB per 100 feet. This is the attenuation of the cable at the highest frequency of interest for the system (usually 300 or 400 MHz). However, cable attenuation is not constant and changes with both frequency and temperature.

Frequency Variation

Cable attenuation increases with increasing frequency in a nonlinear (exponential) manner. This characteristic is due to the composition of the cable and is called *cable slope* or *cable tilt*, and it must be considered when designing a distribution network.

    Figure 4-2 shows the attenuation change with frequency for a 20 dB length of 0.500-inch cable. Figure 4-3 shows attenuation per 100 feet versus frequency for several different sizes of cable. This graph shows that as cable diameter increases, cable loss decreases, which is why larger cables are preferred for long cable runs. The smaller coaxial cables have more loss, and only short lengths of them are used in drop cables.

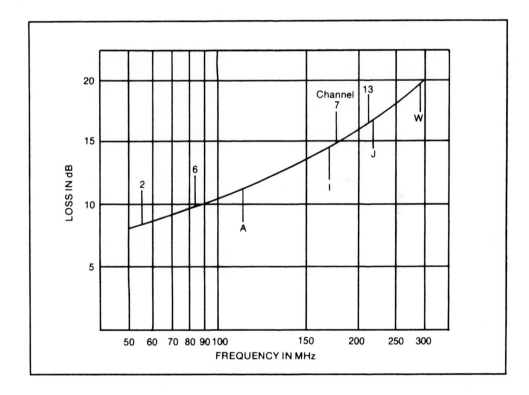

Figure 4-2. 0.500-inch Cable Loss

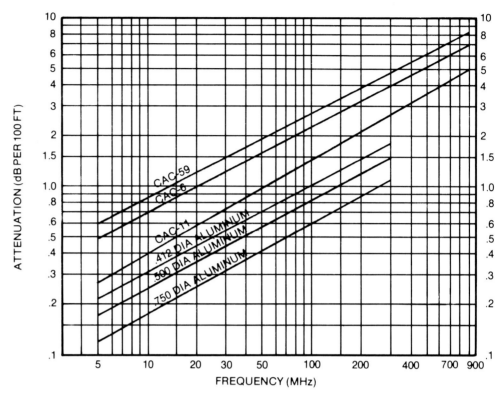

Figure 4-3. Cable Attenuation Versus Frequency for Various Sizes of Coaxial Cable

Temperature Variation

Cable attenuation is also directly affected by temperature variations. The attenuation of coaxial cable increases with temperature at the rate of 0.11% per degree Fahrenheit. This amounts to an overall change of about 15% over the temperature range of -40 to +120 degrees Fahrenheit. The accepted *rule-of-thumb* is 1% change in cable attenuation for every 10 degree Fahrenheit change in temperature at a given frequency.

The network must function properly despite any RF signal level changes caused by frequency and temperature variations. In bidirectional systems there are two different variations that must be considered: one for the forward path and one for the return path. The design must take into account cable tilts for both of these frequency bands. These variations affect the operation of the amplifiers (because they determine equalizer selection and setting) and the overall peak-to-valley response of the system. Amplifiers must compensate for the combination of cable loss, tilt, and temperature variations experienced in daily operation. Proper compensation keeps system gain and signal levels reasonably constant under all possible conditions.

Amplifiers

Because of the parameter variations caused by frequency and temperature changes, only small systems can successfully transport signals without requiring compensation circuitry. Modular amplifiers in the distribution system can include various equalizers, gain blocks, filters, and other circuits that make up for cable-caused variations. *Signal level gain* corrects for attenuation caused by the cable and by other components. *Frequency compensation* (*equalization*) corrects for cable tilt.

Amplifiers used in a broadband network can be divided into four different categories.

▶ Trunk
▶ Bridging
▶ Line extender
▶ Distribution

Each of these types is discussed in the following paragraphs after a description of general amplifier characteristics.

General Amplifier Characteristics

Amplifiers are differentiated by their cost and performance. The cost factor is straightforward: the more expensive units usually provide better performance. The cost of a unit can depend on the following characteristics.

▶ *Gain* is the increase of signal level occurring from input to output of the amplifier. Amplifier gains are usually 20 to 30 dB.
▶ *Output level* is the maximum signal level that the amplifier can deliver.
▶ *Noise figure* is the amount of noise contributed by the amplifier.
▶ *Distortion* is the amount of unwanted modification of the input signal done by the amplifier (this includes intermodulation products, which are often specified separately).
▶ *Gain control* of an amplifier can be either manual or automatic. Automatic gain control units are more expensive.

When evaluating the gain specification of an amplifier, the design engineer should include any associated passive loss. The *usable gain* of an amplifier is the gain available from a fully configured unit and it equals total gain less the insertion loss. A configured unit might contain additional modules such as filters and equalizers. These modules have an insertion loss that must be subtracted from the total gain of the amplifier. This loss is generally between 1 and 3 dB, depending on the configuration of the amplifier.

Amplifier Gain Control

Two different types of gain control for an amplifier are available, manual and automatic.

▶ The gain of a *manual gain control* (*MGC*) amplifier is mainly adjusted by hand. Variations caused by temperature changes can be accommodated automatically by an internal thermal compensator circuit that changes the amplifier's gain. This combination of MGC with thermal compensation suits broadband local network applications, because most of them do not exist in harsh environments. (Amplifiers for outdoor CATV networks must accommodate wider signal level changes found in that environment.)

MGC amplifiers are primarily used on short-range, high-signal-level distribution trunks. Their cost per unit is less than that of automatically-controlled amplifiers.

The thermal compensation provided by MGC units is desirable only when the amplifier is subjected to the same temperature variations as the cable. A problem can arise, for example, if the amplifier is installed in a pedestal above ground and the cable is underground. In that case, the amplifier would probably experience greater temperature variations than the cable. To eliminate possible overcompensation, the thermal circuit should be removed from the amplifier. In most cases, doing so requires no special tools or training.

▶   The *automatic gain control* (*AGC*) amplifier maintains a relatively constant output level regardless of input level variations. It can accommodate changes of 3 dB above or below the nominal input value. When used properly, AGC amplifiers can provide constant signal levels to all outlets in facilities that experience varying environmental conditions.

A general *rule-of-thumb* is that a 6-dB change in the input signal of an AGC amplifier causes a 1-dB change in its output signal.

Types of Amplifiers

Four main types of amplifiers are used in broadband systems: trunk, bridging, line extender, and distribution amplifiers. Each offers different characteristics, performance, and features, and each is appropriate in different applications. These amplifiers are further described in the following paragraphs.

Trunk Amplifiers

Trunk amplifiers are high quality, low distortion units capable of being cascaded into long chains to distribute signals throughout a large geographic area. Amplifiers are *cascaded*, or connected in series along the trunk cable, to make up for losses and variations encountered in long cable runs.

Trunk amplifiers are typically operated at 22 dB gain, with input levels of 8 to 10 dBmV and output levels of 30 to 32 dBmV for 35-channel systems with 20 amplifiers in cascade. Where fewer amplifiers are cascaded, output levels can be increased up to +45 dBmV. When any amplifier is to be operated above its suggested output level, the manufacturer should be consulted for advice.

A *rule-of-thumb* for cascading amplifiers is that each time the number of amplifiers in series is doubled, the output level of each unit must be reduced by 3 dB from its rated output. For example, the output level of each amplifier in a cascade of two units should be 3 dB below the rated output of the amplifiers, or less. Doubling the number of amplifiers in series up to four requires that the maximum output level be reduced to 6 dB below rated output, or less. With eight units in cascade, the maximum output level should be 9 dB below rated output, or less.

Bridging Amplifiers

The bridging amplifier, or *bridger*, provides high level signals for distribution on the branch or feeder lines. They can be installed inside the same housing as the trunk amplifier. The output signal level of a bridging amplifier is usually $+47$ dBmV at the highest operating frequency.

A bridging amplifier receives its input signal from the tap of a directional coupler connected to the output of a trunk amplifier. One to four output lines are available for distribution.

In a broadband network, a common trunk line can feed several buildings. The bridging amplifier can drive distribution cables that feed the individual buildings. With this approach, trunk amplifier levels can be adjusted to CATV standards, allowing easy cascading and future expansion.

Figure 4-4 illustrates an example of signal levels for a trunk and bridging amplifier combination. Return path signal levels, when not given on the drawings, are equal to or slightly greater than the forward path signal levels.

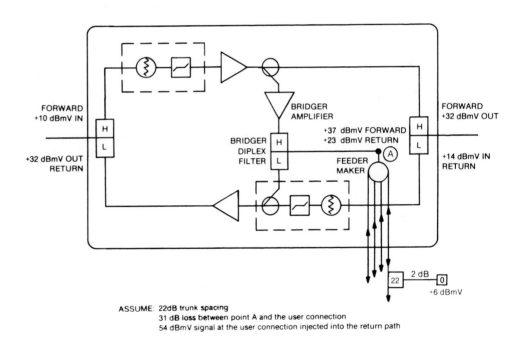

ASSUME: 22dB trunk spacing
31 dB loss between point A and the user connection
54 dBmV signal at the user connection injected into the return path

Figure 4-4. Trunk and Bridging Amplifier

Test points are provided at both the input and output points of the amplifier. The input test point is used to sample the signal before the input filter, pad, and equalizer modules. The output test point is used to sample the signal after the amplifier, directional coupler, and filter sections.

The terms input side and output side are relative to the direction of signal transmission. The input side of an amplifier in the forward path corresponds to the output side of an amplifier in the return path, and vice versa.

Line Extender Amplifiers

Line extender amplifiers, or line amplifiers, are used when the signal level provided by the bridging amplifier is insufficient to drive receiving devices. These amplifiers cost less but have higher distortion and noise figure specifications than trunk and bridger units. Line extender amplifiers should be limited to a maximum cascade of three to provide acceptable quality signals to the users.

Some smaller two-way networks use line extenders as their only amplifying device. Such systems have the following characteristics.

▶ Cascades of three or less

▶ Many outlets located within a small area

▶ Coverage of a limited geographical area

Line extender amplifiers are available in the subsplit, midsplit and highsplit formats for two-way applications, as well as in dual cable versions.

Internal Distribution Amplifiers

Internal distribution amplifiers are high gain units used for signal distribution. They can be used where several high level feeder legs are required, for example, over several floors within a building. Cascading is not recommended because of their higher gain.

One advantage of such amplifiers is that they have built in 110-Volt ac power supplies and do not require ac power to be transmitted over the cable. Currently these amplifiers are available in subsplit and midsplit versions only.

Amplifier Module Additions

There are several additional circuit modules that can be included inside amplifier housings. These modules can provide signal attenuation, return channel gain, frequency equalization, and remote control.

Attenuators

When the input signal amplitude is too high, a pad can be installed inside the amplifier module, in series with the amplifier's input, to reduce the level.

Bidirectional Amplification

All four types of amplifiers can be used in bidirectional networks by adding appropriate filters and a second amplifier module for the return path. Return path amplifiers usually have less gain (19 to 26 dB) than forward path amplifiers since cable attenuation at the lower frequencies (return direction) is less than at the higher frequencies (forward direction).

Equalizers

Variable equalizers to compensate for cable tilt can be installed in each amplifier housing. These circuits provide a frequency response that is the inverse of the response of the coaxial cable. The combined effect of the cable and the equalizer is to provide equal attenuation to all signals regardless of their frequency.

Adjustable equalizers can accommodate different cable lengths. A single equalizer circuit can be used inside all amplifier housings, which only needs to be adjusted for the length of cable between it and the previous amplifier.

Feeder Disconnect

A feeder disconnect circuit can be added into an amplifier housing, usually a bridging amplifier. This circuit permits disconnection of a feeder line from the trunk, either remotely or locally, which can help when troubleshooting and repairing the network.

▶ When noise or unwanted signals are entering the system from an unknown point, disconnecting one feeder line at a time can help to isolate the source of the problem.

▶ When aligning the system, disconnecting branches from the trunk can help to check and match the signal levels coming from all branches.

Control signals for feeder switching originate at the headend and are generated by status monitoring systems and intelligent amplifiers. The state of each module (on, off, or remote), can be selected individually. Placing the module in the on or off state connects or disconnects the feeder and trunk. In the remote state, a signal sent from the headend controls feeder switching.

Power Supplies

All amplifiers require ac power. The internal distribution amplifier contains its own power supply, and can connect directly to a 110-Volt ac outlet. All other units run on either 30 or 60 Volts ac that is delivered over the coaxial cable by power supplies. Distributing power in this manner eliminates the need for 110-Volt ac outlets at each amplifier location and allows greater flexibility in amplifier placement.

Thirty-Volt power is used mostly in older systems. Sixty-Volt power is used widely in modern broadband communication networks.

AC power is coupled to the coaxial cable through devices called *power combiners*. These devices permit the injection of power in either or both directions with little effect on the radio frequency signals.

Once power is delivered to the cable, multi-taps and amplifiers can control its distribution.

▶ For safety reasons, multi-taps pass current along the trunk connections but prevent it from reaching the outlets. Each outlet is electrically isolated from the main network and from other outlets, reducing the possibility of total system failure from accidental or malicious causes.

▶ Amplifiers can pass or block ac power travelling on the cable. Power can be passed to other amplifiers or stopped at either the input or the output of each unit.

Observe these precautions when sending ac power over coaxial cable.

▶ AC power should not be injected through multi-taps or couplers incapable of passing power. Typically, units unable to pass power have F-type connectors.

▶ Use only cables with seamless aluminum shields to convey power.

▶ Consider the current-passing capabilities of each device in the network to ensure that limits are not exceeded.

In system design, a general *rule-of-thumb* has been one power supply for every three amplifiers and cable spans. This quantity depends on cable resistance and amplifier operating current and voltage. Large networks require calculations using power supply voltage and current capacity, amplifier current draw and required input supply voltage, and cable loop resistance. The power available for each amplifier can be found by Ohm's law. These calculations will show where additional power is required.

One result of calculating power requirements is learning that amplifiers are voltage dependent and not current dependent. If the voltage drop across the cable between an amplifier and its power supply is too great, the amplifier operates poorly if at all. To solve this problem, another power supply can be added to the system, or a cable with less resistance can be installed.

Standby power units can be incorporated into any broadband network. These units provide power when the network's main ac input line fails. *Surge protection* gives each unit some protection from high voltage spikes that can occur when power is applied.

Clean and reliable ac power should be used when available. One source of such power is the source used for a computer room, which is also a good location for the broadband network's headend equipment and its power supplies. Such sources often have backup units to ensure that the computer does not fail during a general power failure.

Figure 4-5 shows a typical power connection scheme for a power supply in a broadband network.

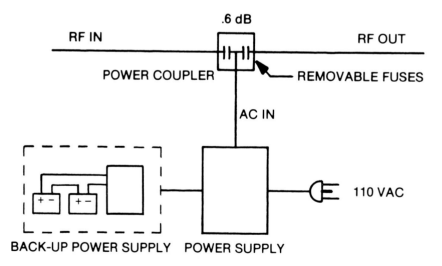

Figure 4-5. Power Supply Configuration

Grounding

Grounding the system at every amplifier helps to ensure long, reliable service. When ground connections deteriorate, amplifiers can be damaged because of high shield current developed from the electrical system's neutral line. All ground points should be checked at least once each year and ground resistance readings taken to ensure system integrity. Make no assumptions about the quality of existing grounds. Verify that the cable system has at least one good ground by measuring existing grounds or by making your own ground. For details on grounding aspects, the Grounding Principles* booklet by Copperweld is recommended. Further information on grounding can be found in appendix I.

Passive Components

This section describes the passive components used in broadband networks. Passive components require no power to operate and include connectors, couplers, splitters, taps, filters, outlets, and terminators.

All passive components cause a certain amount of signal loss when they are inserted in a network. Unlike cable attenuation, which varies exponentially with frequency, this RF signal loss is constant across the entire frequency spectrum and is called *insertion loss* or *passive loss*. The amount of insertion loss is different for each type of device and is specified by the manufacturer. For example, couplers and taps can have insertion losses between 0.4 to 2.9 dB, depending on the tap value. Sample insertion loss values are shown in figure 4-6.

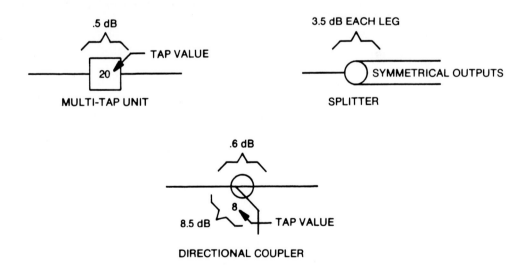

Figure 4-6. Insertion Loss Values

---

* Copperweld Bimetallics Group, Robinson Plaza 2, Pittsburgh, PA 15205, 412/777-3000.

Connectors and Hardware

Solderless 75-ohm connectors designed for each type of cable are the most important components in a broadband system. Industry experience has shown that 75% of all system failures are directly or indirectly caused by connector failure or by poor connector installation.

Connectors come in many varieties from many manufacturers. It requires care to select connectors suitable for the coaxial cable being used and for the environment in which they are used.

A wide range of mounting hardware for the cable and for other components is available from many vendors. Connectors are weak points in the distribution system, and should not be subjected to physical stress by supporting equipment with only the cable. Equipment should never be physically supported by the coaxial cable. The cable and the system components (amplifiers, multitaps, directional couplers, and power supplies) should be separately and securely fastened as the situation dictates. Shrink tubing should be used where connectors enter equipment to ensure the integrity of the connector and to prevent corrosion. Where splices are made in underground installations, materials are available that can be installed over the splice to provide a watertight seal.

Figure 4-7 shows some of the types of connectors currently on the market. Appendix J provides further details on connectors, their parts, and how they attach to equipment.

Directional Couplers

The directional coupler has three ports:

- ▶ Trunk Input (placed toward headend)
- ▶ Trunk Output (placed away from headend)
- ▶ Tap

The main cable attaches to the two trunk connections in the appropriate direction. The branch cable connects to the tap point, and receives only a portion of the signal at the trunk input terminal. Signals originating from devices connected to the tap point are also attenuated by the directional coupler, and always flow toward the headend (to the trunk input terminal of the directional coupler).

The directional coupler provides a means for both dividing and combining RF signals while maintaining the system's 75-ohm impedance and isolation characteristics. The directional characteristic ensures that signals being transmitted from any network device go only toward the headend, and minimizes the reflection of RF energy back to its source.

Four parameters describe the RF performance of a directional coupler:

- ▶ Insertion loss
- ▶ Tap loss
- ▶ Isolation
- ▶ Directivity

FEED THRU (VSF)

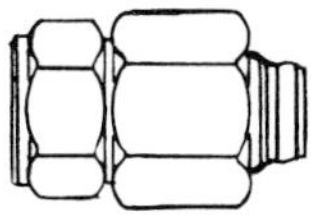

A device that seizes only the outer conductor of the coaxial cable. The cable center conductor extends thru this type connector and is retained within the equipment housing.

PIN TYPE (STINGER)

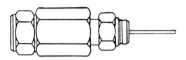

A connector that seizes both the outer and center conductors. This device has an additional feature not found in the feed thru type consisting of a solid brass pin which seizes and retains the cable center conductor. The pin then extends thru the body and is retained within the equipment housing.

SPLICE

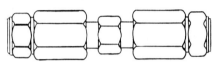

This connector is utilized to join together two cables. It seizes both the outer and center conductors (as in the pin-type).

F FEMALE

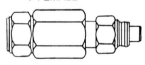

A device used when an F type female port is required at the end of the cable. This connector seizes both the center and outer conductor of the coaxial cable.

F MALE

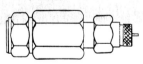

This device is used when it is necessary to have an F type male connection at the end of the cable. This connector seizes both center and outer conductors of the cable.

CABLE TERMINATOR

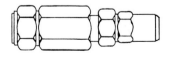

This connector is used in a cable system where it is necessary to terminate both RF signal and 60 Hz AC power. This device seizes the center and outer conductors.

Figure 4-7. Connector Types

Figure 4-8 illustrates the applicable parameters for the directional coupler and for the splitter. In broadband applications, high isolation alone is not the most important parameter. Directivity, which is the difference between isolation and tap loss, is the significant parameter.

All coaxial devices that combine or split signals use the principle of the directional coupler. During installation the directional coupler must not be installed backwards. Doing so would create reception problems at that point and transmit signals in the wrong direction. Arrows indicating signal flow direction are stamped on all devices.

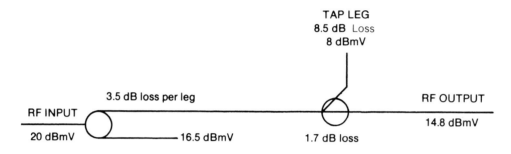

(a) Typical Signal Levels

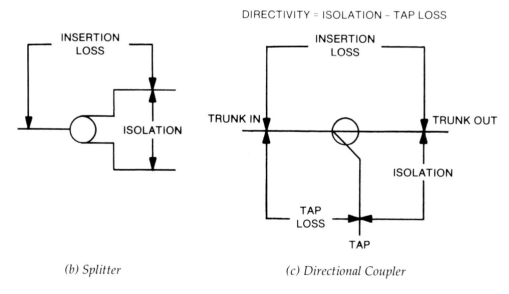

(b) Splitter   *(c) Directional Coupler*

Figure 4-8. Directional Aspects in Cable Systems

Multi-taps

A multi-tap combines a directional coupler with a signal splitter, and allows the connection of several drop cables to the system. Multi-taps are placed along the feeder cables to provide connections to outlets, or to provide access to the network for strings of single-port taps which loop from office to office. Insertion loss between the trunk input and trunk output connections is low. A greater attenuation exists between the trunk input and the tap output lines.

There can be two, four, or eight separate tap connections, called *ports*, from a multi-tap. By changing the tap assembly, the number of ports or their attenuation value can be easily changed without disconnecting the entire multi-tap from the cable. Knowing the length of cable between the port and the outlet it feeds, the attenuation of the port can be selected to allow matching the total attenuation of each path from the headend to each outlet in the system. In addition, multi-taps provide isolation so that all outlets stand alone. Connecting or disconnecting a device on one tap does not affect the operation of the overall system.

Components in distribution legs are usually adjusted to deliver relatively flat levels at the middle of the branch, so that most outlets receive a relatively flat signal. Cable tilt makes it difficult, if not impossible, for all outlets to have a flat signal level across the entire frequency band. Most systems operate properly with a signal level variation of 3 dB above and below the nominal level at any outlet.

Figures 4-9 and 4-10 show a multi-tap and its use in a typical distribution system and signal levels at each tap.

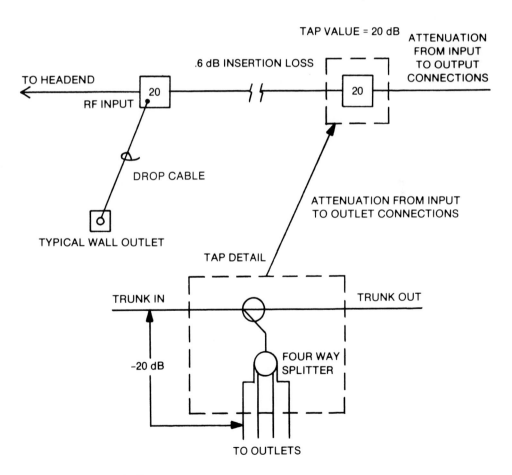

Figure 4-9. The Multi-Tap

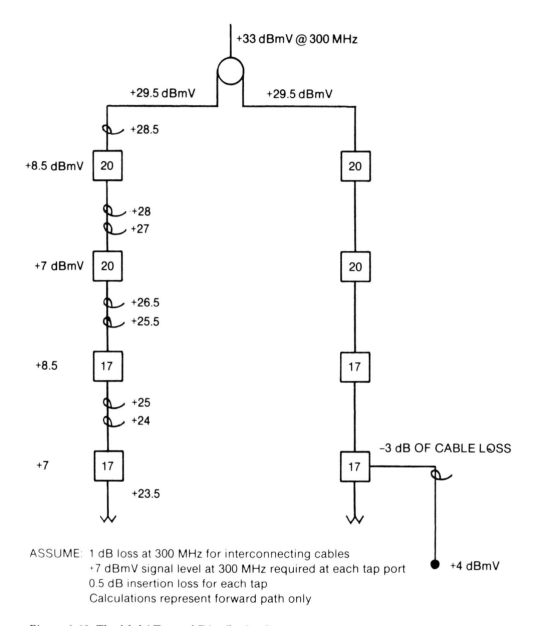

ASSUME: 1 dB loss at 300 MHz for interconnecting cables
+7 dBmV signal level at 300 MHz required at each tap port
0.5 dB insertion loss for each tap
Calculations represent forward path only

Figure 4-10. The Multi-Tap and Distribution Legs

Programmable Taps

Manually-programmable four-way directional taps featuring security traps are now available. Unlike normal and computer-controlled taps, the manual tap accepts any of three plug-in modules to program each port for:

▶   Basic Service

▶   Full Service

▶   Termination

Modules available in the future will allow each port to be individually programmed for one, two, or three pay channels. These taps are useful in CATV networks, but are rarely used in broadband local network applications.

Filters

Filters are used in several applications in most RF systems. Most filters located at the headend combine or separate frequency bands associated with antennas, channel processors, and two-way filter/combiners.

Bandpass filters (*BPF*) pass an assigned portion of the spectrum and attenuate signals at frequencies above and below that passband.

Bandstop filters (*BSF*) attenuate signals in a given frequency range and pass all others.

Diplex filters (*diplexers*) are used in two-way single cable networks. They direct signals in the two frequency bands (high and low) to the correct processing equipment, and have three connections. One is the *common port* and the other two are for the frequency bands associated with the return and the forward paths (*high port* and *low port*). Signals of both these frequency bands appear at the common port.

Diplex filters are used at the input and output of each amplifier housing used for two-way communication over a single cable. Signals from the headend are passed by the diplexer to the forward amplifier and isolated from the return amplifier. Signals from network-connected devices are passed from the diplexer to the return amplifier and isolated from the forward amplifier. The diplexer limits the amount of cross-modulation and intermodulation associated with two-way interactive systems. Envelope delays associated with diplex filters are easier to handle in the midsplit format than in the subsplit format.

Figure 4-11 gives typical frequency response plots for these filters.

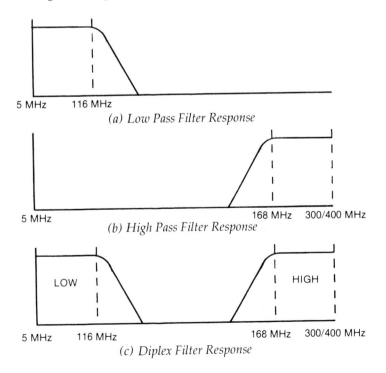

(a) Low Pass Filter Response

(b) High Pass Filter Response

(c) Diplex Filter Response

Figure 4-11. Amplitude/Frequency Response of Typical Filters

Outlets

The wall outlet can be a a single gang plate with two female F connectors mounted back-to-back (called a barrel connector), or with a self-terminating outlet that automatically terminates when the attached device is removed from it. Alternatively, the outlet can be a directional coupler which has only one tap. This allows offices to be wired through a looping coaxial cable, with the tap available to the user and the through portion available to connect to adjacent office taps.

All unused outlets should be terminated by manual insertion of a 75-ohm terminator, or by using self-terminating outlets. Terminating all unused outlets can significantly limit the ingress of undesired signals in the return path. When using manual termination, ensure that the terminator is attached to the outlet plate with a chain or a stainless steel cable. Manual termination is the most positive means to control ingress.

Terminators

Termination of distribution lines or unused tap ports is important to provide proper matching, to maximize power transfer, to limit reflections, and to minimize ingress of undesired signals. Simply stated, a terminator converts RF energy to heat.

Seventy-five-ohm terminators come in several varieties. They are available for both indoor and outdoor applications. Where 60-Volt ac is on the coaxial cable, the ac-blocking type must be used.

Figure 4-12 shows the two symbols that are used to designate terminators.

AC BLOCKING TERMINATOR   RESISTIVE TERMINATOR TYPE

Figure 4-12. Terminator Symbols

Factors Affecting System Design

Introduction

This chapter provides details on planning, designing, and implementing a vendor-independent broadband local area network (LAN). This information covers the tasks performed and the vocabulary used by the designer. It includes guidelines to assist the network manager during the design phase.

The network manager must be aware of the factors considered when a broadband network is designed. However, it is not necessary for a manager to have a detailed understanding of these factors; the broadband design engineer brings that expertise to the project. The manager should know enough about networks to communicate effectively with the technical personnel. The engineer then designs a system that solves the problems described by the manager. This chapter does not provide a list of procedures to follow to design a network. It does identify and describe important design factors. More specific information can be obtained from the cable design group with any major broadband LAN equipment vendor.

Any broadband or CATV-based network should be designed by a qualified coaxial system engineer. When a company uses its own telecommunications department to design a network, a broadband system consultant should review the design and equipment specifications. Such a review is recommended because system layout is a craft that relies on repeated trials and comparisons, rules-of-thumb, and experience.

A major advantage of a properly-designed network is that it can be easily expanded. Systems built according to sound principles several years ago can be upgraded smoothly to support new services, greater traffic, and new communication devices. Without proper design, it is much more difficult to change and expand the existing system.

The contents of this chapter cover five main areas.

▶ The initial approach to a network, including structure, layout, and frequency and bandwidth requirements.

▶ Sample design calculations including signal levels, noise levels, and distortion.

▶ Reliability factors to be considered in network design.

▶ Headend design.

▶ Typical system specifications.

Initial Considerations

Consider the following factors at an early stage in the design of the local area network.

▶ *The information utility*. Keep in mind the idea that a broadband network is an information distribution utility. Like any utility, it should be planned, designed, and installed independently of any specific application that it might support.

▶ *Future expansion*. When construction is underway or when new services are being added to a facility, consider installing coaxial trunk cables, even if there is no current need for a network. These cables can be used to build a broadband system in the future.

▶ *Geographical coverage*. Determine the maximum geographical extent of the system, including a good estimate of future requirements.

▶ *Building survey*. Inspect underground vaults, building access points, ceiling construction, and wall composition. This inspection can aid in designing the layout and can help a contractor provide a realistic cost estimate of the project. Local building contractors can do the building survey. Specialized Engineering Contractors (ECs) can provide total turnkey service including proposals, surveys, design, installation, alignment, and maintenance. Some or all of these services can be used when considering any large broadband network.

▶ *Network architecture and topology*. Determine the general plan for the system.
  ▷ Single or dual cable.
    For single cable select subsplit, midsplit, or highsplit.
  ▷ Main trunk routing.
  ▷ Star, ring, or bus architecture for data transmission devices.

▶ *Frequency allocations*. Select services to be carried and make frequency assignments so that future expansion can be easily done.

▶ *System headend*. Locate the headend centrally within the system. Criteria such as serviceability and network management could dictate a different placement. Adequate space should be available for signal processing, data translation, and test equipment.

▶ *Antenna siting and cabling*. When broadcast television is part of the system, carefully plan the location of receiving antennas and the routing of cables. The construction and alignment of antennas can be difficult and dangerous. Safety is the main concern; operating and performance characteristics are secondary.

▶ *Trunk design*. Make a preliminary layout of system trunk cabling. The best arrangement for a multiple trunk distribution system is to use several trunks radiating from the central headend.

▶ *Redundancy, reliability, and repair*. Consider reliability and repair requirements during system design. This will minimize the need for expensive redundant components to ensure network availability.

   Status monitoring systems and redundant components can be installed in any network. However, redundancy often does not pay for itself unless the system was poorly designed or poorly installed in the first place. Systems that have been properly designed and certified after installation have had few problems.

Some of these factors are discussed in greater detail in this and other chapters of this overview.

System Structure

The structure of a network must be determined early, for this has an effect on many other network design factors. Most commercial and industrial broadband systems have a tree architecture. This versatile form of organization permits data to move between any two points in the system. It readily accommodates all coaxial cable based systems and does not require switching to establish connectivity between any subset of users.

System structure also involves selecting a single or a dual cable system. If single cable is chosen, the frequency division scheme can be subsplit, midsplit, or highsplit. The interface devices that operate together determine the network topology of a channel, which can be bus, ring, or star. Chapter 3 of this overview discusses the major aspects of system structures.

System Frequency Considerations

The highest operating frequency of the system can be 300, 400, or 450 MHz. Today, most systems are designed for 300 MHz, although 400 MHz systems are becoming more widespread. Regardless of the system's design bandwidth, all passive components should be able to pass signals from 5 to 400 MHz. Amplifiers should be able to pass any signals in the system's spectrum.

To determine the necessary bandwidth for a system, draw up a *frequency allocation chart*. Such a chart shows the services occupying each frequency band and helps to ensure that there are no conflicting frequency assignments. The frequency allocation chart in appendix D shows frequencies used in over-the-air transmission and in CATV transmission. This chart can be a good starting point when assigning frequencies for a broadband network.

A general procedure for making a frequency allocation chart includes the following steps.

1. Identify the needed services that can be provided by the network.

2. Estimate the number of users of each service, and calculate the required resources:

    Operating speed and throughput.
    Number of channels.
    Bandwidth required for each service including guard bands between different services.

3. Evaluate interface equipment from all appropriate vendors that can provide the desired services. Select those devices that satisfy your needs.

4. Assign network frequencies to those services whose interface equipment operates on fixed frequencies and cannot be easily or inexpensively changed.

5. Assign network frequencies to the remaining services whose interface equipment can be used on different frequencies.

Additional bandwidth for the expansion of each service should be reserved. This enables the growth of each service without the need to change existing frequency assignments. Commonly used expansion factors are

▶ Subsplit: 40%

▶ Midsplit: 30%

▶ Dual cable: 40%

For example, the initial design of a midsplit system with 100 MHz of bandwidth available in the forward path should not allocate more than 70 MHz of that bandwidth. If less than 30 MHz is available for the future expansion of such a system, some method for obtaining more bandwidth should be considered at the outset.

Regardless of the system's design bandwidth, all passive components should pass all signals between 5 and 400 MHz. Amplifiers need pass only the required bandwidth for the frequency spectrum and allocation for which they are being used.

Bandwidth Requirements

The bandwidth requirements of a system are based on current and projected services. These services can be divided into the following categories.

▶ Closed circuit television

▶ Data communications

▶ Special services

▶ Broadcast television distribution

Each of these services is examined in the following paragraphs, especially regarding bandwidth requirements.

Closed Circuit Television (CCTV)

Each security monitoring device or educational television channel requires 12 MHz of bandwidth, 6 MHz in each direction.

A typical CCTV application would include a television camera generating a video signal and an optional microphone generating an audio signal. Both of these signals are sent to a modulator. The modulator produces a composite RF signal on a channel in the return band. This RF signal is transmitted to the headend where it is translated into an RF signal at a higher frequency in the forward band. The higher frequency signal is distributed throughout the system. A television receiver can be connected at any point in the network to monitor these video and audio signals.

Data Communications

The bandwidth needed for data communications depends on the services needed, the number of users, and the equipment providing the services. This section provides some details on the types of data communication devices available for broadband networks.

A common use of broadband data communications is to support moderate speed data traffic between many remote terminals and one or more host computers. A bandwidth of 6 MHz can accommodate over 4000 terminals operating on several distinct subchannels with equipment from one vendor. A different application might require continuous access to a data channel. This can be accomplished with fixed frequency, point-to-point RF modems. Such devices made by one manufacturer create 28 dedicated, two-way ports inside a single 6-MHz bandwidth.

Most manufacturers specify the number of data subchannels that occupy a 6-MHz bandwidth. The 6-MHz channel provides a common reference for allocating frequencies on the network. The number of subchannels and their bandwidth inside a 6-MHz slot is different for equipment made by each manufacturer; no industry-wide standards exist in this area as of this writing.

The following paragraphs discuss two categories of interface devices.

▶ Fixed frequency, point-to-point or multi-point modems.

▶ Frequency agile, multiplexed, interactive packet communication units.

Each type of interface device is compatible with existing two-way broadband systems. When the broadband system is to be used as a local area network, additional bandwidth might be necessary to allow both types of modems on the same cable. The major differences between them are

▶ the bandwidth of each subchannel;

▶ the tuning ability of the frequency agile unit;

▶ the method used to access the cable.

These differences determine which device is best suited to an application. Given the number of users of each service and knowing the devices to be used to provide that service, the necessary bandwidth can be calculated.

1. Point-to-Point Modems.

A point-to-point modem operates only on its assigned channel. The operating frequency of each modem is fixed. Only one transmitter can be used on any given channel without interference. Full duplex communication between two points in a translated system requires four distinct frequencies: two for transmitting (one from each location) and two for receiving (one at each location).

Point-to-point devices are best suited for applications requiring a dedicated channel and continuous access to the network. One manufacturer provides such devices using carrier signals every 96 kHz. A 6-MHz bandwidth can contain up to 28 of these dedicated two-way ports.

2. Multiplexed Modems.

Devices that need not have continuous access to the network can be multiplexed together to share a single data subchannel. All units can continuously monitor the channel, but only one device at a time can transmit. Channel access protocols determine which station transmits.

Multiplexed interface units are well-suited for applications where traffic is slow to medium speed and bursty. *Bursty* traffic is characterized by short periods of transmission separated by long periods of inactivity, which is typical of people interacting with computers. Many devices operating in this manner can effectively use a single channel without overloading it, since each transmission is brief.

One type of currently available unit uses carrier signals every 300 kHz. This spacing provides 20 distinct subchannels inside a 6-MHz bandwidth. These units are specified to support 200 asynchronous ports at 9600 bits per second on one such subchannel. A network of 4000 ports would require only 6 MHz.

Special Services

A wide range of services can use the network, with each one consuming some portion of the network's bandwidth.

▶ Local origination signals, such as those from a television studio, require 6 MHz for the forward path and 6 MHz for the return path for each video channel.

▶ High resolution video for closed-circuit television (CCTV) applications can use from 4 MHz to 14 MHz of bandwidth in each path.

▶ Digital control signals using dual frequency coding (frequency shift keying) usually require from 300 kHz to 1 MHz depending on the number of signals and the transmission speed.

▶ A telephone system using frequency division multiplexing (FDM) can accommodate 300 simultaneous conversations by using about 6 MHz in each direction.

The manufacturer's specifications list the bandwidth requirements of each device that uses the network.

Television Distribution

Television signal distribution needs a separate book to be described adequately. For this overview, only a brief discussion is possible. Broadcast signals are captured with antennas and are filtered, amplified, and converted with channel processors. Understanding the placement of towers, the selection of antennas, the interaction of signals, and the specification of filters and signal amplitudes can take years of experience. Designing multiple channel headends that include large arrays of interactive equipment and control circuits is a complex task, best left to experienced broadband design engineers.

In general, 6 MHz is required for each television channel transmitted in the forward direction. An additional 6 MHz in the return path is necessary for each link to a remote studio whose signal must be transmitted over the network.

When the frequency of a received television channel must be changed for cable distribution, care must be taken to be sure that the conversion is not a prohibited type. Some channel assignments cannot be converted to others because of co-channel interference and interaction with adjacent channels. These restrictions can also apply to translating some return channels to forward channels. Consequently, an allocation chart must be made and all frequency assignments must be checked for compatibility.

When television signals are to be transported on the coaxial network, the reports made by the Television Allocations Study Organization (TASO) in 1959 should be consulted. These reports provide details on signal quality and how it is specified. Copies can be obtained by writing to any cable television publication or to the National Cable Television Association (see chapter seven).

Bandwidth Allocation

Integrating a communication system consisting of data, video, and voice equipment manufactured by several companies can be a formidable task. The combination of multiple services can require large amounts of system bandwidth. It is important to estimate the total bandwidth required when designing the network.

When assigning operating frequencies, those subsystems that cannot be obtained with selectable frequencies should be assigned first. Tunable subsystems are then assigned frequencies in the remaining spectrum. Managers making channel allocations should always consider current and projected requirements.

Federal Communications Commission (FCC) regulations must be investigated to avoid using prohibited frequency bands. Although broadband systems are not directly regulated by the FCC or by the Federal Aviation Administration (FAA), certain rules about radiation, restricted bands, and similar matters are generally followed. The network should meet or exceed the technical standards set forth in the FCC rules, Section 15, under the heading MATV systems.

When possible, the use of aircraft frequencies at locations within 60 nautical miles of an airport or a transmitter site should be avoided. This regulation currently applies only to CATV operators with over 1000 subscribers. Designing systems to comply with this restriction can prevent expensive redesign or reconfiguration if similar regulations are imposed on broadband local area networks at a later date. There is no current indication that FCC/FAA compliance will be required for local networks in the near future.

Figure 5-1 shows frequency allocation charts to illustrate bandwidth considerations. Such a chart can be made by first identifying the channels on the system, and then dividing the spectrum into forward, return, and guard bands. When a channel is allocated to a specific service, mark the block directly below that channel number on the chart (as are T8 and T10 in the return path of figure 5-1(a)). Appropriate guard bands should be maintained between channels allocated for different services. Information on necessary guard bands and proper filtering should be available from broadband equipment vendors. When a channel is to be translated from the return path to the forward path, connect the corresponding frequency allocations with a dotted line as shown.

Physical Layout

In a multiple building system, the *design of the physical layout* should never loop a main trunk cable through one building and into another. Instead, the trunk should be run alongside each building. Directional couplers connect the trunk to branches that run inside each building. If one branch is damaged, the other parts of the network can continue to operate. Overall network operation is not affected since each branch is isolated from the others.

Signal distribution inside a building should be divided into independent sectors. A user in one sector should be able to function despite a failure in another sector.

The *number and locations of outlets* should be carefully planned. Allow connections for all potential services including data, television, video, voice, and control. An advantage of coaxial cable is that a single drop cable can support all these services at

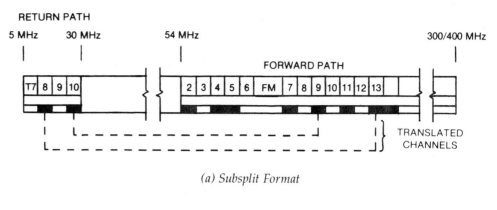

(a) Subsplit Format

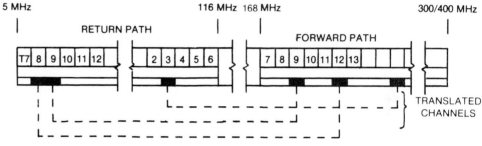

(b) Midsplit Format

CHANNELS ARE GENERAL IN PLACEMENT
AND IN DESCRIPTION

Figure 5-1. Frequency Allocation Charts

one location. When several different devices are to be connected in one office, greater signal strength or multiple outlets must be supplied. For example, if a television receiver and a computer terminal in each office are to connect to the network, two separate outlets should be installed.

Many networks quickly grow beyond the size envisioned by their designers, despite comprehensive planning from the start. In many cases, most of the resources reserved for future expansion were consumed shortly after the initial installation was completed. A limited network forces users to compete for access, creating additional problems. To avoid such problems, the system should be designed to provide full tap coverage (capable of supporting an outlet in each office) and include a 25% expansion factor. This can be done, for example, by reserving one RF port on each 4-port tap for future use. When such expansions are to be done in staggered phases, multi-taps with interchangeable circuit boards are used.

Network branches can also be made expandable. The best approach is to place a splitting device at each major branching point. One port can feed the current network; the other port can be terminated to reserve it for future use. To increase the coverage of the network, new distribution wiring can be installed, checked, and connected to the previously-reserved port. After the new segment has been certified, it can be attached to the expansion port with little or no interruption in network service.

In two-way networks, the *layout of the return paths* is more demanding than that of the forward path. Since the output signals from all return amplifiers eventually converge at the headend, so does all the noise contributed by those amplifiers. The forward path from the headend to any outlet has only the noise build-up of the amplifiers in cascade with one another in that particular path.

In addition, the return path signal levels from all feeder legs at the input of any amplifier must be as equal as possible. A distribution system meeting this criteria can be equalized effectively.

For these and other reasons, the cable loss in each distribution leg should be the same. Note that cable loss was specified here. The passive components can vary in value, number, and location, but the cable lengths should be as equal as possible.

Signal Levels

A reference signal level for the system must be determined. This is the amplitude of the RF signal that appears at each outlet and is measured at the network's highest frequency. It is the value used to design the distribution network and to determine amplifier gain. Maintaining this standard reference amplitude in the entire network produces a transparent distribution system, as described in chapter two. This section describes using the video carrier level as a reference, and how signals with different bandwidths can be related to that reference level.

The Video Reference Level

The most common reference level for a broadband system is the video carrier signal measured in dBmV within a 6-MHz passband.

The video reference level specifies both input and output signal levels:

▶ The amplitude of video signals received at any outlet
▶ The amplitude of video signals injected into any outlet from a transmitting device

By designing the network to convey television signals properly, any other signal level can be related to the video reference level and the proper receive and transmit levels can be calculated for them. Any interface device can be attached to the network, aligned for proper transmit and receive levels, and operated successfully. Each broadband equipment manufacturer uses different signal amplitudes and bandwidths for their interface devices. Establishing a reference level eases the design of a network that uses equipment from several different manufacturers.

The following statement can be used to specify a transparent system.

The broadband system shall provide for the distribution of color or monochrome television signals to any outlet in the system. In addition, the capability to originate television signals from any outlet in the system shall be considered in every design. Other non-television signals shall be compatible with the system for distribution, using a variety of transmission techniques and access schemes. Signals such as data, control, and audio shall conform to the standards set forth for television distribution.

The following values refer to a 6-MHz video signal and satisfy the transparency criteria. These values are used in many operating networks.

▶ The distribution system supplies a signal level of +6 *dBmV* to each outlet. This is the *device receive level*.

▶ The interface device supplies a signal level of +56 *dBmV* to the distribution system. This is the *device transmit level*.

▶ The *forward path loss* is about *50 dB*. (This is the loss from the headend to a typical outlet.)

The receive level is near the middle of the input signal range of a typical television set, which is from 0 to +15 dBmV. Normally, it is desirable to have the receive level between 6 and 10 dBmV at each visual carrier frequency, with the aural carrier level 15 dBmV below the visual carrier level to minimize interference and to provide good reception. The cable network should be designed with all outlet signal amplitudes within 3 dB of each other. This means that the variation from the lowest signal level to the highest signal level at the outlets must be 3 dB or less.

The transmit level of +56 dBmV also originated with television equipment specifications. This is a standard output level for television modulators. The forward loss of 50 dB is found by subtracting the receive level from the transmit level.

Figure 5-2 shows a small portion of a distribution system and how the desired receive level can be obtained at an outlet.

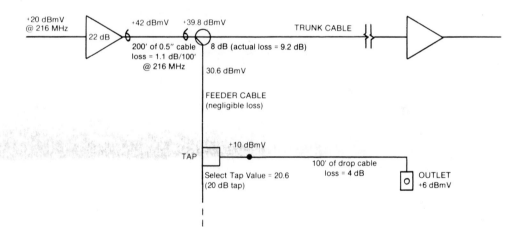

Figure 5-2. Signal Levels from Trunk to Outlet

A different network, providing 35-channel service with a cascade of 20 amplifiers, uses the following levels. (Both network designs are based on a video carrier reference level.)

▶ +8 to +10 dBmV amplifier input level.

▶ +33 to +35 dBmV amplifier output level.

This network has 66-dB rejection of second-order beat frequencies, which is within the range required for good network performance.

Bridging amplifiers for the same channel capacity usually have higher output signal levels (about +45 to +47 dBmV), but fewer such units can be connected in cascade.

Narrow Bandwidth Carrier Levels

Broadband amplifiers are specified in terms of visual carrier levels and 6-MHz video channels (see figure 5-3). When data communications devices with many carrier signals in that same 6-MHz bandwidth are used on the system, the transmission level of each data subcarrier must be lower than the video reference level; otherwise, the amplifiers in the system could be overdriven. This would distort their output signals, and create interfering harmonic signals across the entire frequency spectrum of the cable. The necessary carrier level can be calculated with the following *carrier derating formula.*

DCL = VCL - 10log(NC)
where DCL = carrier level for the desired data signal
VCL = carrier level for a 6 MHz video signal
log = the base ten logarithm
NC = the maximum number of data carrier signals that can occupy a 6-MHz assignment

The level difference between the video and data signal levels depends on the number of data subchannels within a 6-MHz channel. As more subchannels are squeezed into a 6-MHz bandwidth, less gain is available for each signal. The derating formula can be used to determine the maximum signal amplitude for each data carrier, and the manufacturer's specifications should be checked to ensure that this level is adequate for the application.

Two examples using the specifications from two different broadband data transmission units are provided to show how to calculate data carrier levels for a transparent system.

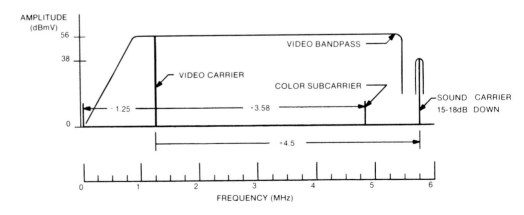

Figure 5-3. A Typical Television Channel

Example 1

Distribution system specifications:

Typical output VCL	= +56 dBmV
Typical input VCL	= +6 dBmV

Manufacturer's specifications:

Data subchannel bandwidth	= 300 kHz
Number of carriers inside 6 MHz	= 20 carriers

Find the typical input and output DCL.

$$DCL = VCL - 10\log(20)$$
$$= VCL - 13 \text{ dB}$$

Typical output DCL = +56 - 13 = +43 dBmV

Typical input DCL = +6 - 13 = -7 dBmV

Given the distribution network's reference levels and this particular interface device, the interface device's transmitter should supply +43 dBmV to the network, and its receiver should expect a -7 dBmV signal from the network. If the interface device cannot be adjusted for these levels, pads could be used or the reference levels could be changed.

Figure 5-4 shows the spectrum of the device used in this example referred to the same 6 MHz scale as the television channel.

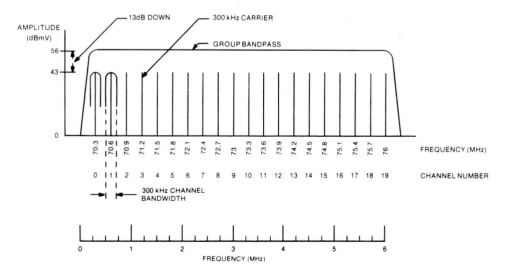

Figure 5-4. A Typical Data Channel

Example 2.

Distribution system specifications:

Typical output VCL	$= +56$ dBmV
Typical input VCL	$= +6$ dBmV

Manufacturer's specifications:

Data subchannel bandwidth	$= 96$ kHz
Number of carriers inside 6 MHz	$= 56$

$$DCL = VCL - 10\log (56)$$
$$= VCL - 18 \text{ dB}$$

Typical output DCL $= +56 - 18 = +38$ dBmV

Typical input DCL $= +6 - 18 = -12$ dBmV

Comparing these two examples confirms that when more subchannels are used in the same 6-MHz bandwidth, the signal levels must be lower for equivalent quality transmission. Using the interface device's specifications, proper signal levels for use on a transparent system can be computed.

Figure 5-5 shows the relationship between signal levels and bandwidths for a television channel and for the two data channels discussed in the two examples.

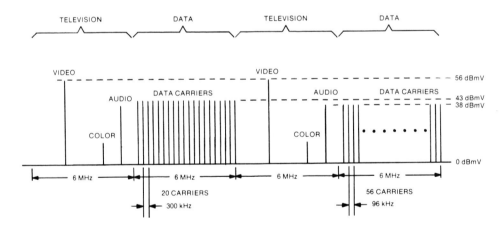

Figure 5-5. Television and Data Carriers

Narrow Bandwidth Advantages

The previous two examples show that many narrow bandwidth data subchannels can be transmitted in a 6-MHz channel without interference by reducing their carrier amplitudes below the video carrier reference level. Two consequences of using narrow bandwidth signals arise.

▶ A narrow bandwidth signal can operate successfully with a lower signal-to-noise ratio. This is because noise increases with bandwidth. The noise floor of the 300-kHz-wide data channel is -70 dBmV, while the noise floor of a 4-MHz-wide television channel is -59 dBmV.

▶ Lower amplitude data signals create less intermodulation distortion than higher-level television signals.

Basing the system's design on video signal levels allows the construction of a transparent network that supports a wide range of interface equipment. Using the carrier derating formula provides the proper signal levels for operating each device.

In addition to channel bandwidth, noise is an important factor in determining operating levels. The following section discusses thermal noise and how it affects signal levels.

Noise Level

Thermal noise is generated by any device operating above a temperature of absolute zero. The amount of thermal noise generated is a function of bandwidth and temperature. For a television system with a 75-ohm impedance and operating at 68 degrees Fahrenheit, a channel with a 4-MHz bandwidth has a *noise floor* (the minimum noise level possible) of -59 dBmV. A 300-kHz-wide channel on the same system has a noise floor of -70 dBmV. The following equation gives the noise floor of a system with a bandwidth B.

$$E_n = -125 + 10\log(B) \text{ dBmV}$$

Appendix E has details on the source of these figures and of other calculations used in this section.

Noise Figure

The *noise figure* of an amplifier is the amount of noise that it contributes to signals that it amplifies. It is a property of the amplifier and cannot be changed by alignment. Increasing the signal level at the amplifier's input changes the *carrier-to-noise* (C/N) *ratio*, but does not change the amplifier's noise contribution. An amplifier with a noise figure of 7 dB raises the noise floor of the 4-MHz system from -59 to -52 dBmV. In a cascaded system, the noise contributed by the amplifiers increases by 3 dB every time the number of amplifiers is doubled. The following table lists noise figure for several values of cascaded amplifiers.

Table 5-1.
Effect of Cascading Amplifiers on Noise Figure

Amplifiers in Cascade	System Noise Figure (dB)
1	Catalog spec. of amplifier
2	Catalog spec. + 3 dB
4	Catalog spec. + 6 dB
8	Catalog spec. + 9 dB
16	Catalog spec. + 12 dB
32	Catalog spec. + 15 dB

This relationship can also be expressed in the following equation:

$$F = F_0 + 10\log(N) \text{ dB}$$

where F = noise figure of the system including all amplifiers

F_0 = noise figure of one amplifier

N = number of amplifiers in cascade

Also, the noise floor of a cascaded 4-MHz system can be computed with

$$E_n = -59 + F_0 + 10\log(N) \text{ dBmV}$$

System Carrier-to-Noise Ratio

Carrier-to-Noise (C/N) ratio is the difference between the input signal level and the noise floor. For an input signal of 10 dBmV, the C/N ratio of the single-amplifier example system (with amplifier noise figure of 7 dB) is 62 dB.

To calculate the C/N of a cascaded trunk system, use the following rule: the C/N ratio decreases by 3 dB every time the number of amplifiers is doubled. This can be stated mathematically in the following formula (derived in appendix E).

$$C/N = C/N_0 - 10\log(N)$$

where C/N = the C/N ratio of the system including all cascaded amplifiers

C/N_0 = the C/N ratio of one amplifier

= -Noise Floor + Input Level - Noise Figure

N = the number of amplifiers

For a system with 32 amplifiers in cascade, a 59 dBmV noise floor, a 10 dBmV input level (typical), and a 7 dB noise figure, its C/N can be calculated as follows.

$$C/N = 62 - 10\log(32)$$
$$= 62 - 15$$
$$= 47 \text{ dB}$$

For convenience, the CATV/broadband industry has related the following C/N values to subjective evaluations of picture quality (table 5-2). A system's C/N ratio should be greater than or equal to 43 dB. The worst case value is measured at the farthest point of each branch.

Table 5-2.
Picture Quality for C/N Values

C/N (dB)	Picture Quality Rating
45	Excellent, no distortion
35	Fine, distortion just perceptible
29	Passable, distortion perceptible
25	Marginal

Noise at a Splitter/Combiner

The effects of noise in a bidirectional network are not identical for both directions. One factor contributing to the difference is the passive signal splitter. This component divides one signal travelling in the forward direction into two or more signals for distribution along different paths. In the return direction, this device works as a *combiner*. It combines signals from two or more paths into a single signal for transmission to the headend. The following discussion describes what happens at a splitter.

▶ Forward Direction

Figure 5-6 (a) shows two carrier signals at the common port of a splitter, and the resulting signal and noise levels that appear at each leg. The same output spectrum appears at both output legs. The carrier signals at frequencies F_1 and F_2 are decreased in amplitude by 3 dB. The noise level is also reduced by 3 dB.

▶ Return Direction

Figure 5-6 (b) shows two different carrier signals, one at each of the two input legs of the combiner. Each carrier signal is attenuated by about 3 dB after passing through the device on its way to the headend.

Noise, however, is a different matter. To calculate the worst-case condition, assume that noise at input port A is in phase with noise at input port B. The noise from each leg is attenuated by 3 dB after passing to output port C. Since the components making up the noise in both paths are in phase, they add together at port C. The result is an output noise level that is the same as the input noise level. The result is a decrease in C/N ratio of 3 dB.

For combiners with more than 2 input legs, the attenuation is greater, and there could be a decrease in the noise level at the output leg. However, the decrease in signal level is still greater than that of the noise, so the C/N ratio could be degraded.

For this reason, noise effects in the return path must be considered separately in the design of a cable system. Be sure that the C/N ratio at the headend from the farthest transmitter is adequate for good reception.

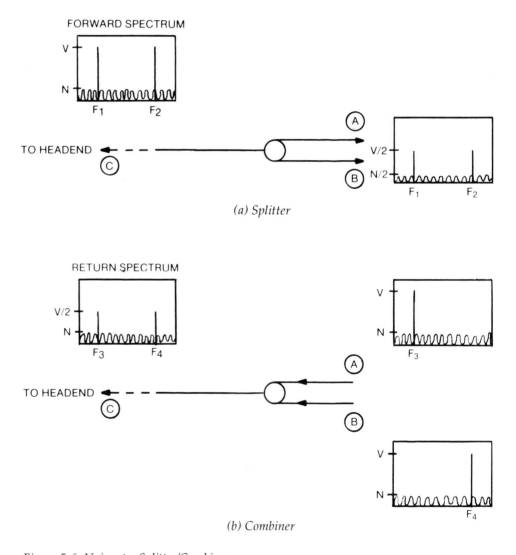

Figure 5-6. Noise at a Splitter/Combiner

Amplifier Selection

Selection of the type of amplifier to use depends on the application, the performance and features desired, the signal level requirements, and the number of amplifiers to be cascaded.

▶ Trunk amplifiers, fitted for midsplit applications, are used in most situations.

▶ Combined trunk/bridger amplifiers are used when the distribution system calls for multiple legs with equal cable loss.

▶ Line extender amplifiers are used only in small networks with little need for future expansion.

Another criteria for selecting an amplifier is the type of gain control used, automatic gain control (AGC) or manual gain control (MGC). Chapter 3 contains descriptions of both types. In small systems, there is little justification for the additional expense of using AGC amplifiers. In larger systems, the expense can be justified and their use improves system performance significantly.

A combination of both AGC and MGC amplifiers is often employed in a large distribution system. When too many amplifiers in cascade have AGC, a noise spike can cause *overcompensation* problems. If the noise spike is large enough, it can decrease the gain of all AGC amplifiers. When this occurs, the amplitude of all desired signals passing through the amplifier is reduced, and the signal-to-noise ratio is severely degraded. A noise pulse lasting several microseconds can cause a loss of desired signals for several seconds

One approach to accomplish AGC has a pilot carrier signal transmitted over the network at a single frequency. The pilot signal is processed by the AGC circuit in each AGC amplifier, which determines the gain of the amplifier. If a noise spike at or near this frequency occurs on the system, amplifier gain drops and data errors or loss of desired signals results. For this reason, AGC amplifiers are often placed at every third to fifth unit in cascade with MGC units. This configuration minimizes overcompensation and provides control over system variation.

AGC is sometimes used in the return path. Special blocking filters and trunk combining considerations require careful design and component selection to control return path gain. Use AGC in the return direction only when suggested by the manufacturer of the broadband equipment.

Design and Performance Calculations

This section provides sample calculations of system parameters including amplifier gain, output signal level, C/N ratio, and intermodulation distortion. Although these examples are presented simply, the design of any broadband system requires a great deal of care and RF signal distribution knowledge. Never attempt to design a large or complex system without first obtaining training or help from a qualified RF Systems Engineer. Usually, the design is performed by a qualified engineering contractor, or through the design services offered by the network equipment manufacturer.

Amplifier Gain

Amplifier gain is the one factor that allows the designer to overcome the loss caused by the coaxial cable. *Usable gain* is the amount of amplification the device can supply, less any flat loss associated with its internal modules, and less any reserve gain.

▶ All signals on a single cable system pass through two diplex filters for each amplifier module encountered. The loss through an equalizer module is proportional to the length of cable being equalized; 2 dB is an approximate figure to use in estimates.

▶ *Reserve gain* is a small amount of amplifier gain set aside during the design process to accommodate signal level variations that can arise when implementing and using the network. This gain can be used when the length of an installed cable run exceeds the estimated value used for design calculations.

Amplifier Gain (Forward Path)		
Minimum full gain (catalog specification)		26.5 dB
Diplex filter loss (2 x 0.6)	1.2 dB	
Equalizer loss	2.0 dB	
Reserve gain	2.0 dB	
Total loss		5.2 dB
Usable amplifier gain		21.3 dB

The distribution system will be designed with an amplifier gain of 21.3 dB in the forward path (the return path needs less gain, but the calculation is similar.

Amplifier Cascade

Amplifier cascade is the number of amplifiers connected in a series configuration (one after another) in a trunk system. Since each amplifier contributes some noise to the system, there is a practical limit to the maximum number of units that can be cascaded. To determine the maximum cascade, several factors must be considered such as:

▶ Output level of the amplifiers
▶ System bandpass
▶ The amount of cable loss between each amplifier

In general, the more amplifiers in a cascade, the lower each amplifier's output level should be.

The following calculations show how to determine the minimum number of amplifiers needed to compensate for the signal loss of the longest cable run of a system. The amplifier cascade to use for designing the system (the *design cascade*) is then found by doubling this calculated minimum value (to provide room for expansion).

Amplifier Cascade

Longest cable run (estimated)	1880 feet
Cable loss (0.5-inch cable @ 300MHz) 1880 feet x 1.31 dB/100 feet	24.6 dB
Required cascade over longest run Cable loss / Usable gain 24.6 dB/21.3 dB	1.1 amplifiers
Minimum required cascade	2 amplifiers
Design cascade 2 x Minimum required cascade	4 amplifiers

Amplifier Output Level

Knowing the design cascade allows the calculation of the maximum amplifier output level permitted in that cascade. The amplifier's rated output level (the highest signal level it can deliver without exceeding distortion specifications) should be reduced by 3 dB for each doubling of the number of amplifiers in cascade.

Cascaded Amplifier Output Level

$$S_c = S_0 - 10\log(N)$$

where S_c = maximum permitted output level of each amplifier in cascade (dBmV)

S_0 = rated output level of one amplifier (dBmV)

N = number of amplifiers in cascade

For example, using amplifiers whose rated output level is $+48.0$ dBmV, the permitted output level in a cascade of four units can be no more than 42 dBmV.

$$S_c = 48 - 10\log(4)$$
$$= 48 - 6$$
$$= 42 \text{ dBmV}$$

Based on the above parameters and the design discussion, the sample system has the following design characteristics (table 5-3).

System Noise

Random noise occurs over a wide bandwidth and is associated with a network's amplifiers. Typical noise figures for amplifiers range from 7 to 11 dB. A previous section showed how the noise for a cascaded system can be calculated.

Noise can also be injected from outside sources such as radio transmitters and electrical motors. This type of noise is usually associated with specific frequencies or a particular frequency range.

Table 5-3.
Sample System Design Characteristics

Single cable network, midsplit implemented	
Cable	
Diameter	0.500 inches
Loss per 100 feet at 300 MHz	1.31 dB
Amplifier	
Gain	21.3 dB
Output level	+36.0 dBmV
Input level	+14.7 dBmV
Minimum outlet level across specified spectrum (± 1.5 dB)	+6.0 dBmV

When properly installed, the system should provide a noise floor 40 dB below the video carrier level. This means that the level of noise in the system should be 40 dB or more below the level of the nominal video carrier. When the noise floor is higher, an amplifier might be contributing more than its share of noise, or a portion of the distribution system might not be properly terminated.

Each amplifier contributes some noise to the system depending on its noise figure. To determine if an amplifier is more noisy than it ought to be, the carrier-to-noise ratio of the system can be measured at various points to find the faulty device. This procedure is best done in a logical progression, either beginning at the headend or at the farthest point from the headend, and moving toward the opposite end until the fault has been isolated.

A specific type of noise found in many electrical systems is hum, which is noise at the ac power line frequency (60 Hz). The suggested limit for the *carrier-to-hum (C/H) ratio* for a full system is 40 dB or more. Cascading amplifiers in a system causes the system's C/H ratio to decrease by 6 dB for every doubling of the number of amplifiers. The following example shows how the C/H ratio of a system is calculated, given a C/H ratio for each amplifier of -70 dB and a cascade of 20 amplifiers.

Carrier-to-Hum Ratio	
Suggested limit	≥ 40 dB
$C/H_c = C/H_0 + 20\log(N)$	
where C/H_c = C/H ratio of the cascaded system	
C/H_0 = C/H ratio of one amplifier	
N = the number of amplifiers in cascade	

For example,

$$C/H_c = -70 + 20\log(20)$$
$$= -70 + 26$$
$$= -44 \text{ dB}$$

Intermodulation Distortion

Intermodulation distortion (IMD) occurs when desired signals on the system interact to produce undesired signals. The primary causes are amplifiers operating at improper levels and defective amplifier stages. Either of these situations might cause the unit to operate in a non-linear fashion, which can create IMD.

If F1, F2, and F3 represent frequencies of carrier signals on the system, intermodulation distortion can occur at the following *second-order beat frequencies*:

▶ F1 ± F2
▶ F1 ± F3
▶ F2 ± F3

Interference can also occur at the following *third-order beat frequencies*:

▶ F1 ± F2 ± F3

The recommended limit on second-order intermodulation distortion is 60 dB below video carrier level. In a cascaded system, second-order beat frequency components increase by 6 dB for every doubling of the number of amplifiers in cascade. However, these same interference signals decrease by 6 dB for every 3-dB drop in amplifier output level. As a result, lowering amplifier output level by 3 dB every time the cascade is doubled maintains the same second-order distortion specification. This practice coincides with the recommendation of dropping amplifier output levels when cascading amplifiers to keep system noise levels within specifications.

Another measure of intermodulation distortion on the system is *composite triple beat (CTB)*. CTB is caused by the combination of all possible third-order beat frequencies that occur on the system. Its source is nonlinear effects of system components on transmitted carrier signals. For example, if a system has five carrier signals at frequencies F1, F2, F3, F4, and F5, the possible triple beats on the system are the following.

▶ F1 ± F2 ± F3
▶ F1 ± F2 ± F4
▶ F1 ± F2 ± F5
▶ F2 ± F3 ± F4
▶ F2 ± F3 ± F5
▶ F3 ± F4 ± F5

The combination of all frequencies represented by these triple beat frequencies is the composite triple beat. The recommended limit for CTB is 51 dB or more below video carrier level. CTB increases by 6 dB with every doubling of the number of amplifiers in cascade.

Composite Triple Beat

$$CTB_c = CTB_0 + 20\log(N)$$

where CTB_c = CTB ratio of a cascaded system

CTB_0 = CTB ratio of one amplifier

N = number of amplifiers in cascade

The System Level Graph

A system level graph summarizes many of the design calculations for a broadband network in a graphical manner. This section discusses how such a graph can be made, and describes the sample shown in figure 5-7.

This graph shows the relationship between amplifier specifications (noise figure, rated output level) and system specifications (noise floor, carrier-to-noise ratio, distortion level, and amplifier cascade). It also shows the *operating window* inside which the amplifier's input and output levels must reside.

A graph like this can be used to check that amplifier operating levels are within acceptable ranges and to show what signal margins exist between the operating values and the limits. It can be generated with the following procedure.

1. Starting with a typical amplifier's noise figure (e.g., 8 dB), compute the *equivalent noise input (ENI)* for the system for cascades of 1, 2, 4, 8, and 16 amplifiers. Plot the resulting values of ENI versus cascade.

    a. For a 75-ohm system with a 4-MHz bandwidth, the noise floor is -59 dBmV.

    b. Adding a single amplifier with an 8 dB noise figure gives an ENI of -51 dBmV.

    c. Each doubling of the number of amplifiers in cascade raises the ENI by 3 dB. For example, with two amplifiers, the ENI moves up to -48 dBmV; with four amplifiers, it becomes -45 dBmV.

2. Select a signal-to-noise ratio for the system (e.g., 45 dB). Add this value to the plot of ENI versus cascade to obtain the plot of minimum acceptable input level.

3. Compute the maximum allowable output level for each value of cascade.

    a. Find the rated output of a single amplifier for the desired distortion level from its specifications. This example uses a device with a rated output of +48 dBmV with a CTB of -57 dB.

    b. Plot output level versus cascade; the output level drops 3 dB with every doubling of the cascade to maintain the CTB specification.

4. The operating window for the system using these amplifiers is the area above the minimum input line and below the maximum output line.

5. Compute the maximum allowable gain for each cascade value by subtracting input from output. This value drops by 6 dB with each doubling of the cascade.

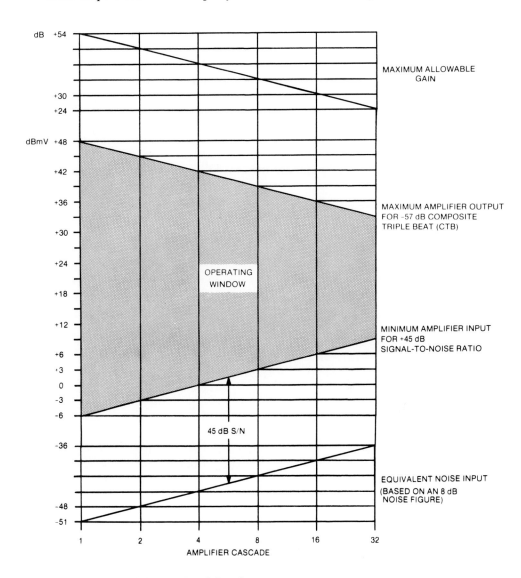

Figure 5-7. A Typical System Level Graph

Using the System Level Graph

A graph developed with the preceding procedure can be used in several different ways. This section provides some ideas.

When designing the network layout, cable lengths cannot always be the desired length for amplifiers to be used at the exact design values. Once amplifier placement is estimated, the loss for which it must compensate can be calculated, and the input level it sees can be found. Plotting this input level on the system level graph provides an estimate of its margin above the minimum input level.

If the calculated input level is below the minimum input level line, the system's S/N specification will not be met at that point in the distribution system, and the design must be modified to provide a higher signal level to this amplifier (e.g., shorten the distance between it and the previous amplifier).

After an adequate input level is delivered to the amplifier, its output level can be determined by adding the amplifier's gain to its input level. The output level should be below the maximum amplifier output level line on the graph; the difference between it and the maximum output value is the margin; 3 dB is commonly used as a minimum margin value.

If the output level is beyond the maximum amplifier output line, the design must be changed to avoid excessive distortion. Possible corrective measures include the following.

▶ Decreasing the input signal level feeding the amplifier input level by introducing attenuators or by inserting more cable between it and the previous unit.

▶ Lowering amplifier gain (but not too far, since trunk amplifiers operate best near their maximum level).

▶ Using fewer amplifiers in cascade.

Reliability and Redundancy

Properly laid out systems cannot have a *total system failure* unless the headend is disabled. Broadband networks are reliable because their design is simple and their components are sturdy. The basic design of a network is very straightforward. The components have been proven in many harsh environments over years of service. For systems that require maximum reliability, redundant components and trunks can be installed to be activated whenever a failure occurs. These backup systems can be switched into the network either manually or automatically by equipment that monitors network performance. This section discusses network reliability and redundancy aspects that can be considered during the design of a broadband network.

The most common causes of system failure in CATV and broadband networks are physical breaks in the cable and faulty connections. Other major causes of failure include power interruptions, processing equipment failures, and interface device failures. Networks inside buildings usually have fewer physical breakdowns but experience the same low number of electronic failures as their outdoor counterparts.

The following paragraphs briefly describe some methods and systems that can increase the probability of the network being operational, including

▶ Installing backup network trunks and amplifiers

▶ Making regular system performance tests

▶ Using automatic monitoring systems and backup switching systems

Broadband Component Quality

The high quality of broadband components is evident from their mean-time-between-failure (MTBF) specifications. The life expectancy of properly installed passive components is estimated to be 30 to 40 years. The MTBF specification of amplifiers, data translators, and video processors is around 18 years.

The reliability specifications of any customer equipment to be attached to the network should be checked, and the appropriate selection should be made based on the network's requirements. Most failures occurring on broadband networks have been related to customer equipment rather than the backbone cable and signal distribution system.

Periodic Maintenance

Passive components require only annual physical inspection and signal tests to insure proper functioning. Once active components are adjusted for proper input voltage, signal level, and equalization, no further adjustment should be necessary. It is recommended to check signal levels at the amplifiers once a year. Usually, no work or adjustment is done, but these yearly checks can provide warnings of possible component failures. CATV alignment and maintenance procedures are much different and are not discussed in this overview.

Equipment Replacement and Repair

Once a device breaks, the failure must be located, the defective unit replaced, and signal levels readjusted when necessary. When a backup device is not available, then replacement of faulty subassemblies should be employed. Enough key components should be kept on hand for this purpose. On-site repair of broken modules is difficult without the proper test equipment and trained personnel. It is often easier and less expensive to send the modules to the distributor or manufacturer for repair.

Redundant Trunks and Components

A break in the cable can usually be quickly repaired at a fraction of the cost of designing and installing a redundant trunk system. When such a short interruption to service cannot be tolerated, a backup trunk cable can be installed. Ideally the primary and secondary trunks would follow different routes. This provides greater reliability but costs more. The secondary cable must be run far enough away from the primary cable to minimize the probability of damage to both cables by a single accident.

Remote-controlled coaxial switches can switch from a primary system to a secondary system if a failure occurs. The secondary system must be checked regularly to ensure that it is working properly. Checking can be done manually or automatically depending on the available test equipment.

If the distribution network is fully redundant but the connected devices such as television monitors, computers, terminals, and cameras are not, then no real redundancy exists. Emergency power sources for key items of equipment should be considered.

Redundancy concerns can be carried too far. For example, a major network not using any form of system redundancy except backup data translators has operated for over five years without a single amplifier, cable, or passive component failure.

Status Monitoring Systems

One approach to controlling backup components and cable trunks is with status monitoring systems. Status monitoring systems that are currently available consist of a computer-based control center located at the headend, and transponders within each amplifier and in key trunk arteries. Each amplifier housing also contains backup amplifier modules. The control unit includes a video display terminal, microprocessor, message modem, and a printer. Such a system can be installed directly into a network, providing the network was designed with status monitoring in mind and uses compatible components.

The control unit interrogates each transponder throughout the day and evaluates the replies received. Any failure triggers the following actions.

▶ The defective area and component are reported on a status board and on the control center's monitor.

▶ The broken module is bypassed and replaced with a standby module. This switching can be done either automatically or on command from the control center. It prevents the loss of communications and allows repairs to be done at a convenient time.

Hardware for this equipment is modular, allowing many existing networks to be upgraded to include status monitoring.

Technical Control Systems

Technical control systems are microprocessor-based control systems that use automated test equipment for system analysis, fault isolation, carrier allocation, and remote feeder switching. A failure in the trunk system can be detected by analyzing responses from control units placed throughout the facility. Once a failure is detected services can be switched from one cable to another, restoring the communication link.

These units differ from status monitoring systems in that they must be custom-built for the network. Status monitoring systems and compatible components are readily available, and can be installed directly into many existing networks. Technical control stations provide remote monitoring and control facilities for any network that has no integrated status monitoring system.

Test equipment found in technical control systems includes programmable spectrum analyzers, signal generators, and sweep oscillators. All these instruments are linked together on a standard IEEE-488 interface bus. A computer program could use a mapping scheme that would show any change in the system's performance based on the original settings and measurements. Detecting an excessive change could trigger alarms and automatic switches if desired.

Total redundancy for two-way systems is not now available, although development seems to be heading in that direction. Both status monitoring systems and technical control stations provide the network manager with valuable information about the network and the ability to control its operation.

Headend Design

The headend is the origin of all RF signals sent to receiving devices connected to the network, and the destination of all signals generated by all transmitting devices on the network. It is the heart of the network, and must be designed carefully so that new services can be added without having to recalculate signal levels and realign amplifiers.

It is a good rule to design the headend and its associated components before designing the remainder of the network. All the passive loss associated with combiners, splitters, and directional couplers can be computed. These computed values then are used to find the signal strength available for distribution throughout the network.

The following paragraphs describe the equipment found in a typical headend. Some aspects of large CATV headends are discussed briefly, since they could be applicable to broadband local area networks in the near future.

System Diagrams

Diagrams of an RF network are provided to show how various needs can be satisfied by a broadband network. Figure 5-8 illustrates a typical headend that can support data communications and one local origination television channel. Signal levels in dBmV are shown at several points. This example is only a guideline but is typical of many headends in use today.

Figure 5-9 shows a typical distribution scheme through a single floor complex. Each office can have its own RF outlet. In addition, the locations of computers, terminals, receivers, and cameras are included.

Standard Headend

A standard headend must be able to support the large bandwidth necessary for a broadband network. Many designers miss this point when designing smaller systems or test bed systems that will be expanded later to support more services. The designer should always plan for the eventual loading of the system. Economizing at the outset by planning for a small network often produces systems that cannot support all the services needed in the near future.

The following paragraphs describe the salient features of figure 5-10, which is a detailed view of a headend.

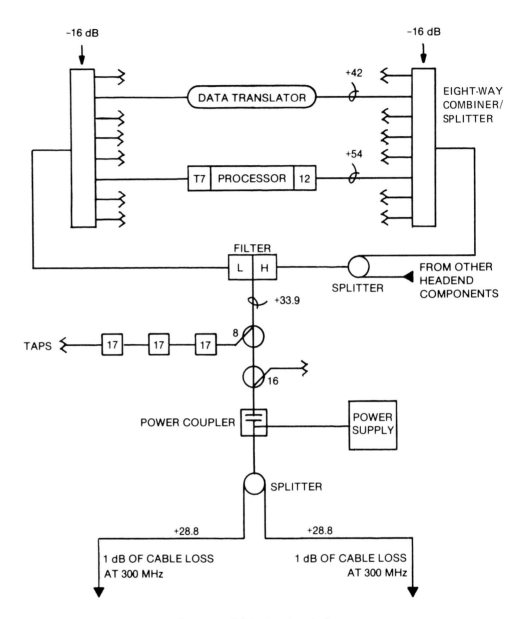

Figure 5-8. Headend Configuration Showing Signal Levels

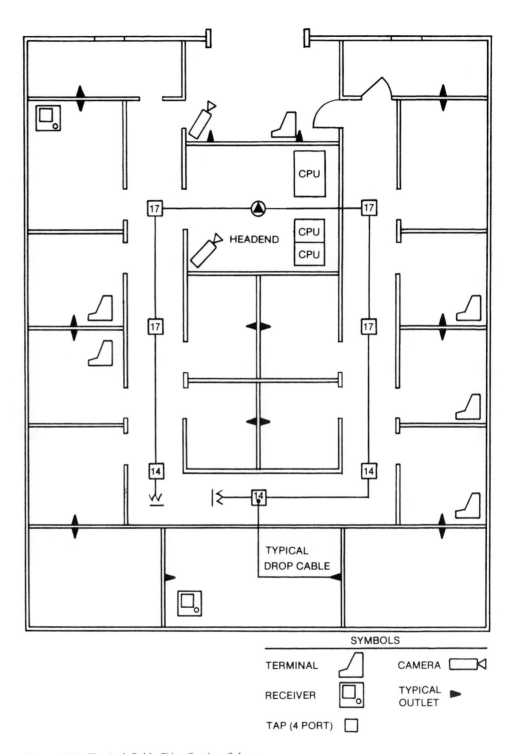

Figure 5-9. Typical Cable Distribution Scheme

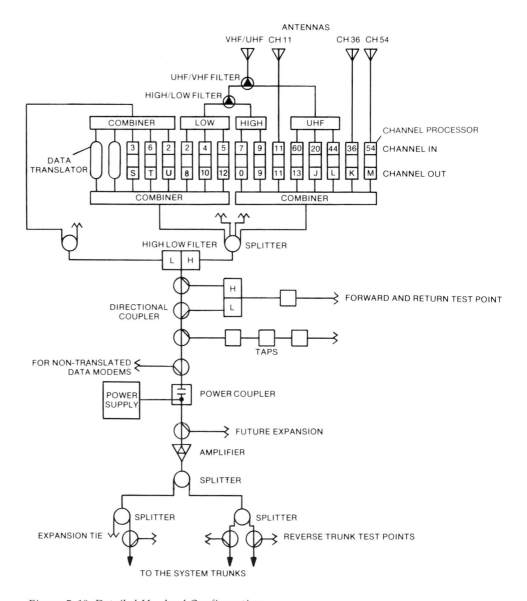

Figure 5-10. Detailed Headend Configuration

First, the top of the drawing shows two *eight-way combiners*. These combiners connect equipment for the various services to the forward and return paths of the system. The example system shown can connect four such combiners in the forward path and two such combiners in the return path. This configuration allows several different devices to be attached to the system at the headend, such as data translators for different data systems, and television signal translators. The number of input connections provided by the combiners is usually proportional to the bandwidth of the path. Using combiners allows the introduction of more services in the future without having to reconfigure the network or to adjust signal levels.

Next, the forward and return frequency bands are processed by a *system filter*. The type of filter used depends on the frequency split chosen.

As with any well-designed communications network, an accessible *test point* is required for test equipment such as a spectrum analyzer.

Two directional couplers are placed back-to-back to support *nontranslated devices*. Non-translated devices are simpler, require no frequency translator, and are less versatile than translated devices.

▶ Non-translated devices are usually restricted to point-to-point or multipoint communications between the headend and remote points.

▶ Non-translated devices connected to different branches cannot communicate directly with each other.

▶ A special headend extension is required if two-way communications to a new location is required; this can cause wiring and signal level problems.

Non-translated systems are not covered further in this book.

A terminated directional coupler provides an expansion point for additional headend devices, or a point for trunk expansion.

The amplifier close to the headend provides needed return path signal gain and return band frequency equalization. At least 75% of all systems require this amplifier to obtain proper signal level at the translator and television processor input connections. This amplifier also brings the return path signals to the input of the data translators at levels that are as equal as possible.

The user should be able to measure the return path signal from each trunk independently. This is accomplished by installing taps in each trunk to monitor the return path's signal. These tap ports are connected to a *test patch panel* where signals from each trunk can be analyzed separately. Both automatic and manual fault isolation are made easier with this configuration.

The broadband system's *power supply* and *power combiner* can be located almost anywhere in the system, although most are placed at the headend. Redundant power supplies and automatic power supply switching units are available if needed.

Additional protective devices should be used at the headend. A *surge protector* and an *RF filter* should be installed on the incoming ac power line. These circuits can protect the equipment from lightning surges, noise, and ground loops that cause hum in the video.

The standard ac voltage level for two-way system design has been 60 Volts. Thirty-Volt systems are less able to supply the proper voltage level to the amplifiers because of voltage drop in the cable. The CATV community has converted most of their systems to 60-Volt operation.

The headend described here is typical of many systems. The flexibility of broadband allows many different system configurations. Just as no two electrical distribution systems are designed exactly the same, no two broadband systems are likely to be identical.

Large CATV Multichannel Headends

Extending the bandpass of coaxial networks to 400 and 450 MHz and increasing the number of available television channels has created unique operating situations. A 400-MHz, 52-channel television system provides significantly more bandwidth than existing 300-MHz 35-channel networks. Using such systems creates new technical problems in design, equipment, and maintenance. These problems apply mainly to CATV networks, but are discussed here since broadband local area networks are planned to provide multiple services and channels.

Composite Triple Beat Distortion

Recall from the previous discussion that composite triple beat (CTB) distortion is the combination of all possible third-order beat frequencies that occur on the system. In a 300 MHz, 35-channel system, analysis of all possible F1 $\pm$ F2 $\pm$ F3 (where F1, F2, and F3 are RF carrier frequencies) triple beats shows that the greatest number of beats falling on one channel is 334 on channel 11 or 12. Because there are so many frequency components so close together, they tend to add on a power basis and appear as narrowband noise on a spectrum analyzer. This impairment can be seen visually on a television picture when the ratio of visual carrier level to CTB level is 51 dB or less.

In a 52-channel system using standard frequency assignments, the greatest number of beats is 842 for channels O and P. To maintain the same -51 dB CTB as in a 35-channel system, all amplifier output levels would have to be lowered by 5 to 6 dB. The combination of lower amplifier gain and higher cable losses at 400 MHz can require the use of more amplifiers and increase network cost. However, by using non-standard frequency assignments, CTB problems can be alleviated. The harmonically related carrier and interval related carrier techniques can be used to control carrier phasing at the headend, and are discussed in the following sections.

Harmonically Related Carrier

One technique used to control large multichannel headends is called *harmonically related carrier (HRC)*. HRC headends use a master 6 MHz generator to phase lock all channels together to retain exactly the same frequency spacing from each other. This generator is called the *comb generator*. With its use, each channel must be shifted by -1.25 MHz, except channels 5 and 6 that must be shifted by $+0.75$ MHz, from their original frequency assignments. This shift results in an additional channel between channels 4 and 5. Implementing the HRC frequency relationship provides an additional 3 to 4 dB of output level and reduces effects caused by CTB. A 44-46 dB CTB would be used as the limiting distortion factor.

The 6-MHz oscillator, however, creates interference problems for frequencies with strong broadcast stations. In the past this problem was solved with phase locking at the channel processor. Phase locking cannot be used in HRC headends because of the frequency shift caused by the comb generator. A similar conflict also arises with frequencies used for aircraft navigation and communication. In some instances, channels on the cable system might have to be abandoned to satisfy offset requirements of the FCC and FAA.

Interval Related Carrier

Another technique used to control multi-channel headends is called Interval Related Carrier (IRC). With an IRC headend, all channels except 4 and 5 operate on the standard NCTA-defined frequencies. (The National Cable Television Association (NCTA) has defined standard frequencies for conveying broadcast television signals over cable systems.)

Channels 4 and 5 are shifted to fall within the spacings of other channels. All but these two channels can operate coherently (on the same frequency as the broadcasted signal) with off-air television channels as part of an IRC cable system. The result is that an IRC system has fewer channels affected by the ingress of off-air signals. An IRC system still allows the same 3-4 dB increase in amplifier output level as an HRC system.

A table in appendix D provides a listing of frequency assignments for each channel for both HRC and IRC systems.

Drawing Standards

Drawings are important tools when building a local area network. Without them, troubleshooting can be extremely difficult and expansion can be a troublesome chore instead of the simple matter that it should be. The following list includes some of the items that should appear on every broadband system drawing to ensure consistency throughout the industry.

1. Symbols used and the part number(s) of the associated equipment. Appendix C provides a recommended symbol chart.

2. System design frequencies, both forward and return.

3. Cables selected and the loss associated with the forward design frequency and the return design frequency.

4. Details of the headend including the calculated output levels of the television processors and data translators, and any equipment limitations regarding power levels.

5. Trunk routing throughout the facility.

6. Calculated length and associated loss for the forward and return directions of each segment of cable.

7. Suggested attenuator values.

8. Suggested equalizers and other necessary equipment for each amplifier.

9. Details regarding ac power distribution and blocking at the headend and at all amplifiers.

10. Distribution system parameters such as tap values, number of ports, and calculated signal levels at each tap.

11. Locations of all manholes, raceways, conduits, trays, and similar structures.

12. Locations of any extra cables for system redundancy or for spares.

13. Suggested trunk and distribution amplifier levels for both the forward and return paths.

14. Minimum outlet and tap levels at the design frequency.

15. A note to terminate all unused outlets when not in use.

16. Recommended alignment method: flat output, flat input, or flat midspan. The flat output method is considered the standard for broadband LANs. All three methods are described in chapter 6.

17. Notes describing any special considerations or special areas of design.

18. A bill of materials.

19. The designer's name, address, and telephone number.

20. A letter that explains the design objectives and parameters, including any special areas needing clarification.

System Specifications

Table 5-4 summarizes the specifications of a typical transparent system. All signal levels are referred to the 6-MHz video carrier level. Each manufacturer should be consulted to ensure that the signal levels are consistent with the requirements of any interface devices to be used on the network.

Table 5-4.
Broadband System Specifications

Carrier-to-noise ratio, forward and return	≥ 43	dB
Peak carrier to p-p hum ratio	< 3	%
Peak-to-valley response, full system	$\pm$ 3.5	dB
Peak-to-valley response, n-amplifier cascade	$1 + n/10$	dB
Peak-to-valley response, any 6-MHz channel	$\pm$ 1	dB
Carrier-to-second order beat ratio	> -60	dB
Carrier-to-composite triple beat ratio	> -51	dB
Outlet receive level, nominal	$+$ 6	dBmV $\pm$ 3.5 dB
Tap receive level, min. (assuming a 2 dB drop cable loss)	$+$ 8	dBmV $\pm$ 3.5 dB
Radiation (measured with a tuned dipole)		
5 MHz to 54 MHz (measured at 10 feet)	15	μV/m
54 MHz to 216 MHz (measured at 100 feet)	20	μV/m
216 MHz to 400 MHz (measured at 100 feet)	15	μV/m
Forward path loss, nominal	50	dB
Return path loss, nominal	46	dB
Headend processor transmit level, nominal	$+56$	dBmV
Headend processor receive level, nominal	$+10$	dBmV $\pm$ 3.5 dB
Data translator transmit/receive levels	Vendor-specified	
Outlet transmit level	$+56$	dBmV

Meeting the following additional specifications helps to ensure proper network operation.

1. Refer all signal levels to the 6-MHz video carrier level.

2. All headend modulators and channel processors should produce an output level of $+56$ dBmV at the input of the forward path combiners.

   These devices should receive an input level of $+10$ dBmV from the return path combiners, within a tolerance of ± 3.5 dB.

3. In office environments, maintain an outlet level of $+6$ dBmV ± 3.5 dB. The tap level is slightly higher than the outlet level to account for drop cable loss).

4. In industrial environments, maintain an outlet level of $+9$ dBmV ± 3.5 dB. This allows the use of a two-way splitter to provide an on-line test point at every network connection. This test point can be used to connect audio modems for maintenance communications (useful when working in remote areas of a large facility).

5. The RF signal level difference between any two adjacent channels should be less than 2 dB.

6. Isolation between any two outlets in the system should be at least 28 dB over the total range of 5 MHz to 400 MHz.

7. For 20 data subchannels within a 6 MHz assignment (300 kHz each), the individual carrier levels should be 13 dB below the peak video level (assuming all carrier signals on).

8. For 56 data subchannels within a 6 MHz assignment (96 kHz each), the individual carrier levels should be 18 dB below the peak video level (assuming all carrier signals on).

9. Any unused outlet should be terminated with a 75-ohm resistor to minimize reflections. This can be accomplished either by attaching a terminating connector to the outlet, or by using self-terminating outlets.

A distribution system including tap values, passive splitter values, and the number and type of connectors, can be designed based on these recommended specifications.

Summary

This chapter has provided information relating to the design of broadband networks. The reader should have gained an understanding of the design process from this material. This understanding should encourage effective communication between the network designer and the network user. The network user should have also gained an appreciation for the complexity of network design, and an awareness of some of the compromises and tradeoffs that require experience and judgment. The next chapter provides details on aligning the completed network so it can provide its specified services.

System Alignment

Introduction

Once a broadband communications system has been installed, it must be aligned and certified before it can be used. If the network's performance is not certified, significant operating problems could occur as communication services are added to it. This chapter provides information to aid the alignment and troubleshooting of both single and dual cable systems. This discussion assumes that the system has been designed properly for two-way communications. The reader should have an understanding of broadband communications as provided by the preceding chapters of this book.

The Need for Alignment

There are two basic reasons for aligning a network.

▶   To provide a flat signal response across the network's bandpass.

▶   To provide equal signal levels at each outlet.

The *alignment process* consists of adjusting the gain and equalizer controls of each amplifier to achieve consistent and desired signal levels throughout the system. Two-way trunk amplifiers are typically adjusted to produce 18 to 22 dB of gain at the system's highest design frequency (300 or 400 MHz), and correspondingly lower gain at lower frequencies. Two-way line extender amplifiers provide higher gain at the cost of greater noise. Amplifier selection depends on system design factors covered in chapter five.

Figure 6-1 shows schematic illustrations of broadband amplifiers for single cable subsplit and midsplit systems and for dual cable systems. These drawings show the relationship of test points, pads, adjustable equalizers, and gain blocks; this information is useful during alignment.

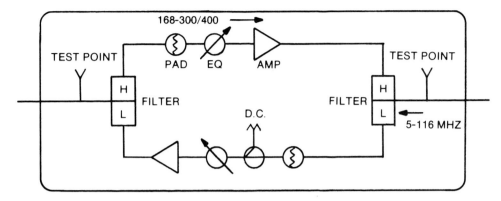

(a.) Midsplit Amplifier

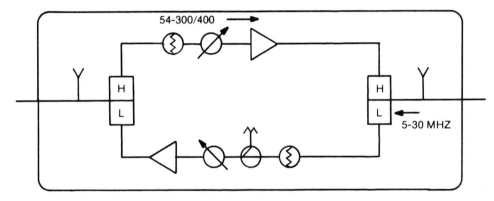

(b.) Subsplit Amplifier

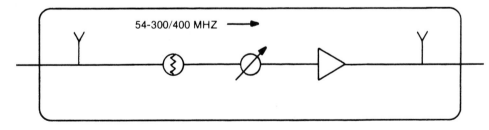

(c.) One-Way Amplifier

Figure 6-1. Trunk Amplifier Configurations

Before aligning the system, it helps to become familiar with the insertion loss of the broadband components used and the expected attenuation characteristics, including tilt, of the coaxial cable(s). Also, it is important to examine the system design drawings, to ensure that they reflect the current installed configuration, and to note any changes made to the design during installation.

Test Equipment Required

This section discusses the test equipment required to align and maintain the system. About $15,000 (at 1983 prices) is required to purchase the appropriate test equipment, including the following items.

▶ RF spectrum analyzer

▶ RF sweep generator

▶ Field strength meter

▶ Multimeter

▶ Cable reflectometer

▶ RF radiation monitor

Appendix F lists some currently available devices that can be used in these applications.

The *RF spectrum analyzer* provides a graphic display of the frequency spectrum and is useful in system alignment, troubleshooting, carrier analysis, carrier-to-noise measurement, intermodulation distortion measurement, and many other performance tests. The spectrum analyzer should have a 75-ohm impedance, and show signal levels in dBmV from 5 to 500 MHz.

An *RF sweep generator* is a signal source. It should have the following characteristics.

▶ RF output signals from 5 to 500 MHz with a tunable sweep function.

▶ A fixed-frequency output signal at any frequency in the bandpass range. The bandwidth of this signal should be adjustable.

▶ Adjustable output signal amplitude.

▶ 75-ohm impedance.

▶ Calibrated for dBmV.

The *field strength meter* (FSM) is a popular test item. This is a tuned RF voltmeter used for determining the amplitude of a signal at a specific frequency. This unit is easy to operate and can be used for measuring performance, aligning amplifiers (once they are equalized), verifying signals, and troubleshooting. It also is calibrated in dBmV and some units can read signals up to 800 MHz.

A *multimeter* is used primarily for checking power supplies and evaluating ground loops. Such units should be portable and able to select several voltage and resistance ranges.

The *cable reflectometer* is used in locating cable faults caused by physical breaks in a given span of cable or by reflections caused by bends or kinks. These instruments can indicate the location of the fault to within a few inches. Cable system troubleshooting time is minimized by the combined use of a reflectometer and accurate, scaled drawings of the cable layout.

A *sniffer* or a *bloodhound* are instruments that measure *RF radiation*. These instruments pinpoint areas where the system radiates RF energy, either through a poor connection or a damaged cable. When radiation occurs, one can also assume that the system is more susceptible to signal ingress. Signal ingress can hinder the proper operation of the network. It is important to ensure that the system provides maximum isolation from external signals, including electromagnetic interference (EMI) and radio frequency interference (RFI).

There are many other types of specialized test equipment that the CATV industry uses. These include devices to do the following functions.

▶ Status monitoring

▶ Feeder disconnection

▶ Automatic fault isolation

▶ Remote interrogation of pre-calibrated RF detectors

These devices are not covered in this overview.

Documentation

Documenting the process of cable alignment is important. A record should include at least the following items.

▶ The tests made.

▶ The equipment used.

▶ The settings on the test equipment.

▶ The signal levels measured.

▶ Miscellaneous items including changes made to the system during alignment, and special notes about any unusual situations.

Producing good documentation will simplify the diagnosis of system problems later. Proper documentation provides a normal pattern for comparison with the abnormal pattern encountered during a breakdown. Noting simple items, such as test equipment settings and readings during alignment, helps maintenance personnel understand the task at hand, and shows what signal levels are expected at various points in the system. Good records allow easy replication of alignment conditions, which can provide a good starting point for troubleshooting.

Coaxial Cable Certification

Separate tests can be done on the cable and the distribution system to help ensure proper performance, and to identify possible problem areas before the network is used for data transmission.

The *structural return loss test* measures cable loss before and after installation.

▶ Sweep testing the cable before installation minimizes the chances of installing defective cable, which could be costly to replace.

▶ Checking the cable after installation points out any frequencies having excessive loss due to handling and attaching connectors.

Small discontinuities in the cable can cause reflections or standing waves. These periodic disturbances can make a very effective filter, resonating at the frequency whose wavelength is twice the spatial period of the discontinuities. This can produce a pronounced spike in the return loss at that frequency. Each individual discontinuity might have a return loss of 60 dB, but the accumulated effect could be enough to cause a narrow-band dip in the transmission characteristic of the cable. When the dip occurs at a desired carrier frequency, the additional attenuation can degrade that channel's response. Sweep testing the cable before and after installation can detect structural problems when poor return loss readings are obtained.

The *cable sweeping* or *component performance test* can be performed during or after installation. A sweep generator at the headend and a portable sweep receiver make up the system. Measurements can be made at any point in the network. This test analyzes and plots system attenuation, cable exponential characteristics, and spectrum integrity through the passive and active components. The performance of the return path in bidirectional networks can be verified in this way. With a sweep test one can compare the characteristics of the installed system to specifications of the designed system.

Alignment Methods

There are three common methods used to align a broadband system.

▶ Flat amplifier output

▶ Flat amplifier input

▶ Flat midspan

Each approach is briefly described in this section. The flat amplifier output method applied to a single cable, midsplit format system is covered in more detail in the following section.

All discussions pertain to MGC amplifiers. Read the manufacturer's manuals on the amplifiers being used, and pay close attention to the sections covering configuration and alignment. These manuals give suggestions on alignment procedures for AGC amplifiers, and advice on proper output levels.

Since cable systems have been designed around the transportation of television signals, the amplitude of television signals are to be used when aligning a system. A system aligned to convey only data carriers can be overdriven and caused to operate in a nonlinear mode when video carriers are introduced. These effects can render the network unusable for television signal distribution. Therefore, it is always recommended to design and align broadband systems to convey television signals.

Flat Amplifier Output

In the *flat amplifier output method*, each amplifier is adjusted to give equal amplitude for signals of all frequencies at its output connection. As a result, each amplifier compensates for the tilt of the cable between it and the preceding amplifier (figure 6-2(a)). This alignment technique is recommended for most broadband systems, since it can be done by one person. Flat output alignment results in a flat response across the spectrum at taps immediately following each amplifier, with increasing variation (tilt) in signal response as the distance from the amplifier's output point increases.

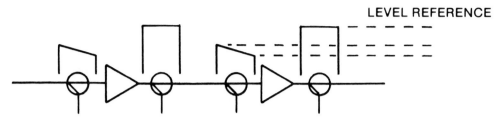

(a) Flat Amplifier Output Alignment

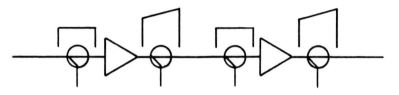

(b) Flat Amplifier Input Alignment

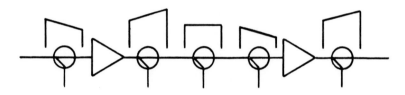

(c) Flat Midspan Alignment

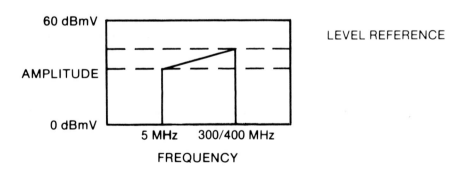

Figure 6-2. Amplifier Alignment Techniques

Flat Amplifier Input

In the *flat amplifier input method*, each amplifier is adjusted to give equal amplitude for signals of all frequencies at the input of the following amplifier in cascade. Each amplifier compensates for the tilt of the cable between its output point and the input point of the next amplifier (figure 6-2(b)). This alignment method requires two people, one at the amplifier being adjusted and one at the measurement point (the following amplifier in cascade). Flat input alignment results in a flat response across the spectrum at taps immediately preceding each amplifier, with increasing tilt in signal response as the distance from the amplifier's input point increases.

Flat Midspan

In the *flat midspan method*, each amplifier is adjusted to give equal amplitude for signals of all frequencies at a point midway between it and the following amplifier in cascade (figure 6-2(c)). This method also requires two people: one at the amplifier being adjusted and one at the measurement point (a tap at the midpoint of the cable between the amplifier being adjusted and the following amplifier). Flat midspan alignment results in a flat response across the spectrum at taps in the middle of each cable span between two amplifiers, with increasing tilt as the distance to either amplifier decreases.

Flat midspan is the best alignment technique because it provides a flat signal response at more outlets than the other techniques provide. The flat output method is used more often because it is easier to do. An alternative combines aspects of both the flat output and midspan procedures (called the *modified flat midspan method*).

1. First, the system is aligned using the flat output method.

2. Then, the signal is monitored at the midpoint between any two amplifiers or between any two multi-tap cable runs (which approximates the location of a typical outlet). The slope control of only the amplifier nearest the headend is adjusted to provide a flat response at the monitored point. If the amplifier has no slope control, the equalizer control is adjusted.

The modified flat midspan method provides flat response near the midpoints of all pairs of amplifiers. Unless all the cable spans are identical in length, some variation from flat response occurs at these midpoints.

Summary

The flat output method is recommended for all trunking situations (that is, for cable spans that have no taps between amplifiers). The flat output method is also recommended for aligning the interior or feeder (as opposed to trunk) distribution system. It could be enhanced by adjusting the slope of the the first amplifier in the system, as described for the modified flat midspan method.

Alignment of Single Cable Two-Way Systems

Alignment of a bidirectional single cable system requires two operations: aligning the forward path and aligning the return path. The following paragraphs describe both procedures done on a midsplit system. The alignment of a subsplit system is similar except for the frequencies involved.

Non-amplified System

Non-amplified system refers to a network that does not use an amplifier, or to the portion of a larger network that is supported only by the headend processing equipment and does not include an amplifier. Such systems normally include the headend taps or local distribution taps connected to the headend.

The non-amplified portion of a network must be aligned for proper signal levels before the rest of the distribution network is aligned. This is because amplifier gain can be increased or decreased to achieve proper levels, while non-amplified sections do not have this additional dimension of control. Headend devices, such as data translators and television channel processors, must be adjusted to provide the proper input signal levels to all devices in the non-amplified part of the network.

Forward Path Alignment

In both subsplit and midsplit systems, the forward and return paths occupy a wide bandwidth. To properly align an amplifier requires observation of several frequencies. The technique described here uses a sweep generator placed at the headend. Its output level is adjusted to the video carrier level listed on the system design drawings or in the system specifications. A spectrum analyzer measures the response of the system at any point. Figure 6-3 illustrates forward path alignment described in the following procedure. Follow proper RF measurement techniques throughout this procedure.

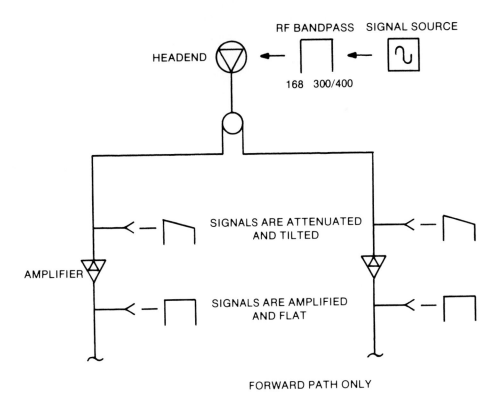

Figure 6-3. Forward Path Alignment

1. Attach the sweep generator to a combiner input port feeding the forward path at the headend.

2. Adjust this generator to supply the desired video carrier level in the forward band (168-300 MHz).

3. Connect the spectrum analyzer to the output of the first amplifier in cascade.

The attachment of the spectrum analyzer to the amplifier is critical. Some amplifiers have built-in test points whose signals are 20 dB below system levels. Others require the use of a test probe that contains a 30-dB isolation pad. Use the proper technique for the amplifiers in the system. Consult the appropriate catalog or manual to find the exact amplifier configuration being used.

---

4. Observe the variations in signal levels between the low and high frequencies of the forward band. Follow the amplifier manufacturer's procedure to set the equalizer controls of the amplifier properly to obtain a flat response across the forward band.

5. Adjust the amplifier's gain until the measured output level matches the specified design level. When additional attenuation is needed, insert an appropriate pad in the forward path until the desired signal level is achieved. A good *rule-of-thumb* is to select the pad value that allows the gain adjustment control to be within 1 dB of its maximum setting. This leaves some headroom that can be used when additional gain is required because of system reconfiguration or cable degradation.

6. Move the spectrum analyzer to each amplifier in turn and repeat this procedure. Where the output level of the amplifier is not noted on the drawing, adjust the amplifier until the desired signal strength is obtained at a typical outlet.

It is possible (but not recommended) to align a system with a field strength meter instead of a spectrum analyzer. Since the meter monitors a single frequency at a time, the sweep signal can be replaced by two or three fixed-frequency pilot signals. The meter can then be used to align the network. This technique usually requires two people: one to change the frequency of the signal source and one to align the amplifiers. Communicating over two-way radios in a large facility can speed this process dramatically. The system should be equalized by comparing the response at low frequencies to the response at high frequencies (170 and 300 MHz).

Return Path Alignment

Aligning the return path is similar to aligning the forward path with a few exceptions. Move the signal source from the headend to appropriate taps or outlets in the network. Adjust this generator to the frequency and amplitude of the transmitting devices that will be connected to the network. Connect the spectrum analyzer to the output of the return amplifier being aligned. Then, adjust the return path equalizer to obtain a flat response at the frequencies of the return path (5 to 116 MHz). The procedure is similar to that for the forward path.

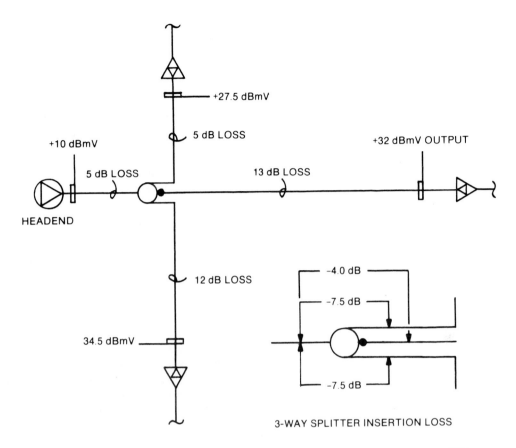

+27.5 dBmV

5 dB LOSS

+10 dBmV

5 dB LOSS   13 dB LOSS   +32 dBmV OUTPUT

HEADEND

12 dB LOSS

34.5 dBmV

-4.0 dB

-7.5 dB

-7.5 dB

3-WAY SPLITTER INSERTION LOSS

NOTE: ALL LOSSES NOTED ARE CALCULATED AT 116 MHz

Figure 6-4. Signal Levels at a Junction

One significant difference between forward and return path alignment is the *addition of signals from different branches* on their way to the headend. The unity gain principle cannot be followed when designing or aligning the return path. Figure 6-4 shows three return path branches being combined, and that the return signal levels from each branch must be the same. Since the length of cable in each branch is probably different, the gain of amplifiers in the three paths must be adjusted to compensate for a different loss. Adjust the gain of each amplifier so that the following amplifier receives equivalent signal levels from each branch. This procedure can be tedious, especially for large systems. However, it is a standard procedure that ensures compatible performance for outlets throughout the network.

Return amplifiers have less gain than forward amplifiers, because there is less cable attenuation at the lower return frequencies.

For example, 100 feet of a typical 0.500-inch diameter cable has a loss of 1.32 dB of signal level at 300 MHz. The same length has a loss of only 0.8 dB at 116 MHz. A section of cable 1000 feet long, would have attenuations of 13.2 dB and 8 dB at 300 MHz and 116 MHz respectively.

Trunk and bridger amplifiers have return path gain controls that operate like the forward path controls. Line extender amplifiers might not have a gain control. When using amplifiers without gain controls, select an appropriate pad to reduce the signal level to the desired value.

An alternative to measuring signal levels throughout the network is to calculate the losses associated with the return path and then make corresponding adjustments of each transmitter connected to the system. If there are large differences in transmitter levels, moving devices throughout the network is difficult; adjustments would be necessary for each device. This approach is not recommended.

Ideally, proper alignment permits the use of pre-adjusted communication devices anywhere in the network. Network services can then be physically moved from one location in the network to another without readjusting the interface device or realigning the network components. In addition, signals introduced into the return path from any location in the network arrive at the headend within 3 dB of each other. A system designed and aligned to these specifications can accommodate all originally installed services and make the addition of new services easy.

Alignment of Dual Cable Systems

Dual cable systems comprise two separate cables. The *inbound cable* carries signals to the headend from the distribution network; the *outbound cable* carries signals from the headend to the outlets. The bandpasses associated with both paths are from 54 to 300 or 400 MHz. A common design practice is to make the outbound path identical to the inbound path, except that the direction of the amplifiers is reversed.

There are some special dual cable systems that use different bandpasses than those listed above. Stocking extra amplifier modules for such systems is recommended, since spare parts cannot always be purchased off the shelf from standard suppliers.

Inbound and Outbound Cables

Alignment techniques for dual cable systems are similar to those listed for single cable systems, except that each cable path is unidirectional. Usually, the inbound cable is identical to the outbound cable.

The most accurate alignment is done by placing a test signal generator at the remote end of the inbound path. Check the signal at each amplifier and adjust its gain until the test signal is received at the corresponding outbound path outlet at the desired level.

Amplifier equalization can also be performed in this manner. Transmit a signal on the inbound cable and monitor it at each amplifier in the distribution system. The frequency response at any location can be checked and adjusted easily by this *round robin method.*

This procedure can also be performed on a single cable system, by following the signals translated by the central retransmission facility. This unit receives return path signals, converts them to the higher forward frequency band, and transmits them on the forward path. The round robin signal level can be monitored at any point in the system.

An alternative to measuring signal levels throughout the network is to calculate the attenuation in each span and adjust the amplifiers to compensate for this computed loss. A *span* is the cable between the two outlets (for inbound and outbound signals) at any one location. As with many alternatives, it is less accurate and should be used only when no test equipment is available. Never use this technique on any large system.

Potential Problems and Solutions

Problems can arise during alignment. Typical symptoms are a loss of signal or an inability to adjust the amplifiers to achieve the desired output. Problems can be divided into the following categories.

▶ Design errors
▶ Installation defects
▶ Hardware failures
▶ Vandalism
▶ Test equipment defects

Design errors can be minimized by following these rules.

▶ Have the system designed by a qualified broadband CATV/LAN engineer.
▶ Double-check all mathematical calculations (this is the most frequent cause of design errors).
▶ Verify that the system's components are used within their design specifications.
▶ Completely test any hardware intended for use in an abnormal or non-standard scheme.

The most common installation defects have the following causes.

▶ Poor connections
▶ Components installed in the wrong direction
▶ Defective amplifiers
▶ Improperly configured amplifiers
▶ Power supply failures
▶ Blown fuses
▶ Cable damage

A common symptom of all the above problems is *little or no RF signal*. RF signal loss often results from *improper tightening* of the cable's center conductor in internally seized cable components. RF signals can radiate across an open path between the two conductors, but the greater attenuation (because there is no solid connection) results in a much lower output signal level. If ac power is on the cable to feed the amplifiers, a good indication of an open circuit is the loss of ac power on the device's output.

If the center conductor is connected too tightly, other problems can occur. *Overtightening* can cause the center conductor to weaken and eventually break.

Incorrect orientation of passive taps can permit signals to pass through the unit with little or no signal strength at the tap ports. On all components, the direction of signal flow (from trunk input to trunk output) is shown by an arrow stamped on the housing. The arrows on directional coupler taps should point away from the headend. In dual cable systems, the arrows should also point away from the headend, for both the inbound and outbound cable paths.

▶   Output ports of forward path amplifiers should point away from the headend.

▶   Output ports of return path amplifiers should point toward the headend.

▶   Output ports of amplifiers in dual cable systems point away from the headend on the outbound path and toward the headend on the inbound path.

Another common installation defect is a *short circuit*. Usually, fuses in the power combiner blow when ac power is applied to a distribution branch containing a short circuit. Another possible symptom is high current draw. This can pull the voltage supplied to the amplifiers down below the required level. Test the supply voltage at each amplifier with a voltmeter. When the amplifier has less than adequate supply voltage, its performance degrades and affects network operation.

Passive equipment is less subject to failure. Most failures concerning these devices are associated with *damage during installation*. The directional couplers used in trunk or branch connections have no tap ports. To verify that ac current is passing through the device, it is necessary to open the cover and measure it with a meter.

One system component that is often overlooked is the *outlet drop cable*. Usually, this is a short piece of coaxial cable with type F fittings on both ends. It connects the interface device to the outlet. Since the cable is directly exposed to the user, or to a potentially hostile environment, damage can occur. A common problem is physical stress placed on the cable by the user or by furniture near the cable. This stress can push the center conductor back into the connector, and cause *intermittent or total loss of signal*. The connected device can fail totally or operate intermittently. The resulting problems can drive the maintenance crew crazy. Such problems can also cast doubt on system operation in general, when in fact most of the system is operating properly.

Broadband network problems can be found quickly by one who is familiar with their effects on the system. However, when several problems occur simultaneously, isolating each one can be difficult. Analyze each problem separately and in a logical sequence. Don't stop once a problem is discovered and fixed. Continue with the cable certification test until it is successfully completed.

Radiation and Signal Ingress

It is important for a system to reject outside interference. When the system leaks or radiates, some external signals must also be entering the system. If these signals are sufficiently large, they can disrupt or inhibit normal network operation.

Measurement of signal ingress is straightforward. Install a signal source at the headend and set it to an amplitude that simulates the level of the strongest signals on the system. Then monitor all points in the system for excess radiation using an instrument for measuring leakage (a sniffer or a bloodhound).

Radiation usually occurs where the network is not mechanically sound, because of poor connections, broken or missing shielding, or extreme kinks and bends in the cable.

The return path is susceptible to unwanted signal ingress that is more difficult to measure. The amount of return path ingress can be related to the amount of radiation measured in the forward path. Excessive signal ingress is often caused by poor connector installation and loose or open equipment housings. Another major cause is the shielding characteristics of the drop cable itself. The highest quality coaxial cable with several shields should be used. The shielding should consist of alternating foil and braid shields. Finally, all unused tap ports and drops should be terminated.

Checking an Outlet

During alignment and troubleshooting, it might be necessary to ensure that an outlet is working. Use the following round robin test to verify that an outlet is functional.

Simulate the operation of a data modem with the following connections. Attach a combiner (two-way splitter) to the outlet to be tested. Connect a signal generator to one side of the splitter and a field strength meter to the other side. Inject a test signal into the system. This signal should be 3.5 dB higher than the output amplitude of the network interface device usually connected to that outlet (to account for the 3.5 dB loss through the splitter). The frequency of this test signal should be within the input bandpass of the data translator (that is, it should be within the return frequency band).

Monitor the translated signal from the original injection point with the field strength meter. The meter should show a signal level that is 3.5 dB lower than the usual level at that outlet, because of the splitter.

Monitoring System Performance

Once alignment is completed and the network is put into operation, system performance should be monitored continuously. Inject a pilot carrier signal at the headend on a reserved frequency. Set its output amplitude to a value which can be monitored throughout the network with a field strength meter or a spectrum analyzer, and install a monitoring device. This reference signal can be checked on a regular basis at a typical outlet in the system, as part of a preventive maintenance program.

Summary

This chapter covered the alignment and troubleshooting of broadband networks in general. Once a network has been designed and installed, its performance must be certified before it can be used with confidence to convey RF signals. Certifying and aligning the network properly will identify any broken, misplaced, or poorly-installed components. Certifying the network at the outset aids later troubleshooting work by providing a record of correct signal levels and frequencies at critical test points for later verification.

This section listed test equipment and described how to use it when aligning and testing the network. The differences between forward and return path alignment were mentioned. Finally, possible network problems and solutions were described, including RF radiation and signal ingress.

For Further Reading

7 For Further Reading

For more information about broadband communications consult the following resources.

▶ The appendices following this chapter contain specific details on some topics that were covered in this book. The bibliography lists reference sources in several areas.

▶ The National Cable Television Association (NCTA) can provide information on technical standards used in the CATV industry.

National Cable Television Association
918 16th St., NW
Washington, D.C. 20006
202/775-3550

▶ The following trade publications can provide useful information in many areas; this list is not comprehensive.

Cable Age
1270 Avenue of the Americas
New York, NY 10020

Cable Marketing Magazine
Jobson Publishing Corp.
16th Floor
352 Park Avenue South
New York, NY 10010

Cable News
Suite 1200N
7315 Wisconsin Ave.
Bethesda, MD 20814

Cable Vision
2500 Curtis St.
Denver, CO 80205

CATJ, The Official Journal
for the Community
Antenna Television Association
4209 N.W. 23rd
Oklahoma City, Oklahoma 73107

Communications Engineering Digest,
The Magazine of Broadband Technology
2500 Curtis St.
Denver, CO 80205

Communications News
124 South First St.
Geneva, Illinois 60134

Data Communications
42nd floor
1221 Avenue of the Americas,
New York, NY 10020

Micro Communications
Miller Freeman Publications
500 Howard St,
San Francisco, CA 94105

Appendices

Appendix A: Definition of Terms

Allocations The assignment of specific broadcast frequencies by the FCC for various communication uses (e.g., commercial television and radio, land-mobile radio, defense communications, microwave links). This divides the available spectrum between competing services and minimizes interference between them. The manager of a broadband network must allocate the available bandwidth of the cable among different services for the same reasons.

Amplifier A device which increases the power or amplitude of an electrical signal. Amplifiers are placed where needed in a cable system to strengthen signals weakened by cable and component attenuation. Two-way, single-cable systems use a forward and a reverse amplifier inside one enclosure to boost signals travelling in both directions.

Balancing Adjusting the gains and losses in each path of a system to achieve equal signal levels (usually to within 3 dB) at all user outlets. A balanced network also provides near equal input signal levels to the headend from transmitters connected anywhere in the network.

Bandwidth The frequency range that a component, circuit, or system can pass. For example, voice transmission by telephone requires a bandwidth of about 3000 Hertz (3 kHz). A television channel occupies a bandwidth of 6 million Hertz (6 MHz). Cable systems occupy 5 MHz to 300 or 400 MHz of the electromagnetic spectrum.

Branch An intermediate cable distribution line in a broadband coaxial network that either feeds or is fed from a main trunk. Also called a feeder.

Broadband In general, wide bandwidth equipment, or systems that can carry signals occupying a large portion of the electromagnetic spectrum. A broadband communication system can simultaneously accommodate television, voice, data, and many other services.

Cable Loss The amount of RF signal attenuation by a given coaxial cable. Cable attenuation is mainly a function of signal frequency and cable length. Cables attenuate higher frequency signals more than lower frequency signals according to a logarithmic function. Cable losses are usually calculated and specified for the highest frequency carried (greatest loss) on the cable.

Cable Powering Supplying operating power to active CATV equipment (for example, amplifiers) with the coaxial cable. This ac or dc power does not interfere with the RF information signal.

Cable Tilt The variation of cable attenuation with frequency. The attenuation of a length of cable increases with frequency; therefore, the amplitude of an RF sweep signal measured at the end of a length of cable is greater at low frequencies than it is at high frequencies. (When viewed on a spectrum analyzer, the waveform tilts downward).

Cable TV Previously called Community Antenna Television (CATV). A communication system which simultaneously distributes several different channels of broadcast programs and other information to customers via a coaxial cable.

Carrier Sense, Multiple Access with Collision Detection A communication medium access technique that allows many separate transceivers to share a single channel. All units monitor the channel (carrier sense), and do not transmit while receiving a signal. Whenever the channel is idle, any unit can transmit (multiple access). If two or more units begin transmitting during the same break, their signals collide and they realize that a problem occurred (collision detection). They cease transmitting and wait for a short time before trying to retransmit the data.

Cascade The number of amplifiers connected in series in a trunk system.

CATV Community Antenna Television (See Cable TV).

Central Retransmission Facility (CRF) The location of the equipment that processes RF signals for network retransmission. Also called headend.

Coaxial Cable A single cable with two conductors having a common longitudinal axis. The center conductor carries information signals; the outer conductor (shield) is grounded for those signal frequencies to prevent interference. This shield is often made of a flexible foil or braid, or solid aluminum. The two conductors are separated by an insulating dielectric.

Composite Triple Beat (CTB) The combination of all possible third-order beat frequencies $(F1 \pm F2 \pm F3)$ that occur on a system.

Composite Video Signal The complete video signal. For monochrome systems it comprises the picture, blanking, and synchronizing signals. For color systems it includes additional color synchronizing signals and color picture information.

CRF Central Retransmission Facility.

Cross Modulation A form of signal distortion in which modulation from one or more RF carrier(s) is imposed on another carrier.

CSMA/CD Carrier Sense, Multiple Access with Collision Detection.

Data Communication Equipment (DCE) Equipment that links a user's data terminal equipment to a common carrier's line (for example, a modem).

Data Rate The rate of information transfer, expressed in bits per second (bps).

Data Terminal Equipment (DTE) Equipment that is the ultimate source or destination of data.

dB Decibel.

dBmV Decibels relative to one millivolt. Zero dBmV is defined as 1 millivolt across 75 ohms.

Number of dBmV $= 20 \log_{10} (V/1 \text{ mV})$

DCE Data Communication Equipment.

Decibel A unit used to express the ratio between two power or signal values:

Number of dB $= 10 \log_{10} (P_1/P_2) = 20 \log_{10} (V_1/V_2)$

where log is the base ten logarithm;

P_1, P_2 are measurements of power at two points;

V_1, V_2 are measurements of voltage at two points having identical impedance.

Directional Coupler A passive device used in cable systems to divide and combine RF signals. It has at least three connections: trunk in, trunk out, and tap. The trunk signal passes between trunk in and trunk out lines with little loss. A portion of the signal applied to the trunk in line passes to the tap line, in order to connect branches or outlets to the trunk. A signal applied to the tap line is attenuated and passes to the trunk in line, and is isolated from the trunk out line. A signal applied to the trunk out line passes to the trunk in line, and is isolated from the tap line. Some devices provide more than one tap output line (Multi-taps).

Distribution Amplifier A high gain amplifier used to increase RF signal levels to overcome cable and flat losses encountered in signal distribution.

Drop Cable A flexible coaxial cable which connects a network tap to a user's outlet connector. Also called Drop Line.

Drop Line Device Any external device attached to the coaxial network through a drop line (e.g., RF modem, television set, audio modulator).

DTE Data Terminal Equipment.

Echo See Reflection.

Equalization A technique used to modify the frequency response of an amplifier or network to compensate for distortions in the communication channel. The ideal result is a flat overall response. This slope compensation is often done by a module within an amplifier enclosure.

F Connector A standard, low cost, 75-ohm connector used by the CATV industry to connect coaxial cable to equipment.

FDM Frequency Division Multiplexing.

Feeder Cable See Branch.

Feedermaker A splitting device used to provide multiple outlet connections from distribution amplifiers.

Filter A circuit that selects one or more components of a signal depending on their frequency. Used in trunk and feeder lines for special cable services such as two-way operation.

Flat Loss Equal signal loss across the system's entire bandwidth, such as that caused by attenuators.

Flooded Cable A special coaxial CATV cable containing a corrosion resistant gell between the outer aluminum sheath and the outer jacket. The gell flows into imperfections in the aluminum to prevent corrosion in high moisture areas.

Forward Direction The direction of signal flow in a cable system that is away from the CRF or headend.

Frequency The number of times a periodic signal repeats itself in a unit of time, usually one second. One Hertz (Hz) is one cycle per second. One kilohertz (kHz) is one thousand cycles per second.

Frequency Division Multiplexing (FDM) Dividing a communication channel's bandwidth among several subchannels with different carrier frequencies. Each subchannel can carry separate data signals.

Frequency Response The change of a parameter (usually signal amplitude) with frequency.

Frequency Translator See Translator.

Harmonic Distortion A form of interference caused by the generation of signals according to the relationship Nf, where N is an integer greater than one and f is the original signal's frequency.

Headend The facility that contains a cable system's electronic control center, generally the antenna site of a CATV system. It usually includes antennas, preamplifiers, frequency converters, demodulators, modulators, and other related equipment which receive, amplify, filter, and convert broadcast television signals to cable system channels. It might house a host computer in broadband data communication systems.

    In two-way broadband systems, the headend holds at least the frequency translator.

High Frequencies Frequencies allocated for transmission in the forward direction in a midsplit broadband system, approximately 160 to 400 MHz.

Highsplit A frequency division scheme that allows two-way traffic on a single cable. Reverse path signals come to the headend between 5-174 MHz; forward path signals go from the headend between 232-400 MHz. No signals are present between 174-232 MHz.

Hub Same as a headend for bi-directional networks except that it is more centrally located within the network.

Inbound The cable carrying signals to the headend in a dual cable system.

Insertion Loss The loss of signal level in a cable path caused by insertion of a passive device. Also called Thru Loss.

Isolation Loss The amount of signal attenuation of a passive device from output port to tap outlet port.

Low Frequencies Frequencies allocated for transmission in the return direction in a midsplit broadband system, approximately 5 MHz to 116 MHz.

Main Trunk See Trunk Line.

MATV Master antenna television system. A small cable distribution system usually restricted to one or two buildings.

Mid Band The part of the electromagnetic frequency spectrum that lies between television channels 6 and 7, reserved by the FCC for mobile units, FM radio, and aeronautical and maritime navigation applications. This frequency band, 108 to 174 MHz, can be used to provide additional channels on cable television systems.

Midsplit A frequency division scheme that allows two-way traffic on a single cable. Reverse path signals come to the headend between 5-116 MHz; forward path signals go from the headend between 168-400 MHz. No signals are present between 116-168 MHz.

Modem A modulator-demodulator device. The modulator codes digital information onto an analog carrier signal by varying the amplitude, frequency, or phase of that carrier. The demodulator extracts digital information from a similarly modified carrier. It allows communication to occur between a digital device (for example, a terminal or a computer) and an analog transmission channel, such as a telephone voice line.

Multi-tap A passive distribution component composed of a directional coupler and a splitter with two or more output connections. See Tap.

Noise Any undesired signal in a communication system.

Noise Figure A measure of the amount of noise contributed to a system by an amplifier.

Noise Floor The minimum noise level possible on a system. A 4-MHz-wide channel on a 75-ohm cable system operating at 68 degrees Fahrenheit has a noise floor of -59 dBmV.

Outbound The cable carrying signals away from the headend in a dual cable system.

Outlet See Tap Outlet.

Packet Communication Unit (PCU) A device that connects a terminal or computer to a broadband packet-switched communication network.

Pad A passive attenuation device used to reduce a signal's amplitude.

Receiver Isolation The attenuation between any two receivers connected to a cable system.

Reflections Secondary signals caused by the collision of the transmitted signal with structures or objects in its path. Such echoes can be created in a cable system by impedance mismatches and cable discontinuities or irregularities. Also called echoes.

Reserve Gain An amplifier has a maximum amount of available gain. When designing a network, amplifiers are specified to supply this maximum amount of gain less some amount of reserve gain. This reserve gain can be used to accommodate signal level variations that can occur during installation. A common figure used for reserve gain is 2 dB.

Return Loss A measure of the degree of impedance mismatch for an RF component or system. At the location of an impedance mismatch, part of the incident signal is reflected back toward its source, creating a reflected signal. The return loss is the number of decibels that the reflected signal is below the incident signal.

Return Path Reverse direction; towards the headend.

Signal Level The RMS voltage measured at the peak of the RF signal. It is usually expressed in microvolts referred to an impedance of 75 ohms or in dBmV.

Slope The difference between signal levels at the highest frequency and at the lowest frequency in a cable system. Also called spectrum tilt.

Slope Compensation The action of a slope-compensated gain control. The gain of the amplifier and the slope of amplifier equalization are changed simultaneously to provide equalization for different lengths of cable; normally specified in terms of cable loss.

Spectrum Tilt See Slope.

Splitter A passive device that divides the input signal power from the forward direction into two or more output signals of less signal power. Input signals from the reverse direction are combined into a single signal and passed toward the headend. Splitters pass through 60 Hz power to all lines.

Subsplit A frequency division scheme that allows two-way traffic on a single cable. Reverse path signals come to the headend between 5 and 30 MHz; forward path signals go from the headend between 54 and 400 MHz. No signals occupy the 30 to 54 MHz band.

Surge Arrestor A device that protects electronic equipment against surge voltage and transient signals on trunk and distribution lines.

Tap A passive device, normally installed in line with a feeder cable. It removes a portion of the signal power from the distribution line and delivers it to the drop line. The amount of power tapped off the main line depends on the input power to the tap and the attenuation value of the tap. Only the information signal (and not 60 Hz power) goes to the outlet ports. See also Multi-tap.

Tap Outlet A type F connector port on a tap used to attach a drop cable. The information signal is carried through this port. The number of outlets on a tap usually varies from two to eight.

Termination A 75-ohm resistor that terminates the end of a cable or an unused tap port with its characteristic impedance to minimize reflections.

Thru Loss See Insertion Loss.

Tilt See Slope (spectrum tilt) or Cable Tilt.

Time Division Multiplexing (TDM) Sharing a communication channel among several users by allowing each to use the channel for a given period of time in a defined, repeated sequence.

Translator In a two-way broadband system, an active device at the headend which receives RF signals coming to it from devices connected to the network, converts them to signals at a higher frequency, and sends them back to the network in the forward direction.

Trunk Amplifier A low distortion amplifier that amplifies RF signals for long distance transport.

Trunk Cable Coaxial cable used for distribution of RF signals over long distances throughout a cable system. Usually the largest cable used in the system.

Trunk Line The major cable link(s) from the headend (or hub) to downstream branches. Also called Main Trunk.

Unity Gain A design principle wherein amplifiers supply enough signal gain at appropriate frequencies to compensate for the system's cable loss and flat loss (Cable Loss + Flat Loss = Amplifier Gain). It implies the use of identical amplifiers separated by identical lengths of cable.

Usable Gain The amount of gain an amplifier can supply after subtracting any loss due to its internal modules, and any reserve gain.

Appendix B: Abbreviations and Acronyms

A	amplifier input level in dBmV	Hz	Hertz; 1 cycle per second
ac	alternating current	IMD	intermodulation distortion
AGC	automatic gain control	IRC	interval-related carriers
AM	amplitude modulation	ITFS	instructional television, fixed service
amp	amplifier		
B	bandwidth	kHz	kilohertz; 1,000 cycles per second
C	amplifier cascade factor; 10log(NC)		
		LAN	local area network
C/H	carrier-to-hum ratio in dB	MATV	master antenna television
C/N	carrier-to-noise ratio in dB	MGC	manual gain control
CATV	Community Antenna Television	MHz	megahertz; 1,000,000 cycles per second
CCTV	Closed-Circuit Television	modem	modulator-demodulator
CRF	central retransmission facility	mux	multiplexer
CRT	cathode-ray tube	mV	millivolts
CSMA/ CD	carrier-sense, multiple access with collision detection	N	number of amplifiers in cascade
CTB	composite triple beat	NC	number of data carriers in a 6-MHz channel
dB	decibel	NCTA	National Cable Television Association
dBm	decibel referred to one milliwatt; 0 dBm = 1 mW		
		PA	public address
dBmV	decibel referred to one millivolt; 0 dBmV = 1 mV	PCU	packet communication unit
		RAM	random access memory
DC	directional coupler	RFI	radio frequency interference
dc	direct current	RJE	remote job entry workstation
DCL	data carrier level	ROM	read-only memory
E_n	noise level, noise floor	R/WM	read/write memory
EMI	electromagnetic interference	RF	radio frequency
ENI	equivalent noise input in dBmV	S	amplifier output level in dBmV
F	noise figure	s	seconds
F1,F2	carrier frequencies on a system	S/N	signal-to-noise ratio
FAA	Federal Aviation Administration	TDM	time-division multiplexing
		TVRO	television, receive-only
FCC	Federal Communications Commission	UHF	ultra-high frequency; 300-3000 MHz
FDM	frequency-division multiplexing	μV	microvolts
		V	Volts
FM	frequency modulation	VCL	video carrier level
FSK	frequency shift keying	VHF	very-high frequency; 30-300 MHz
G	amplifier gain		
GHz	gigahertz; 1,000,000,000 cycles per second	XLTR	translator
		XM	cross-modulation distortion
HRC	harmonically-related carriers		

Appendix C: Broadband Symbols

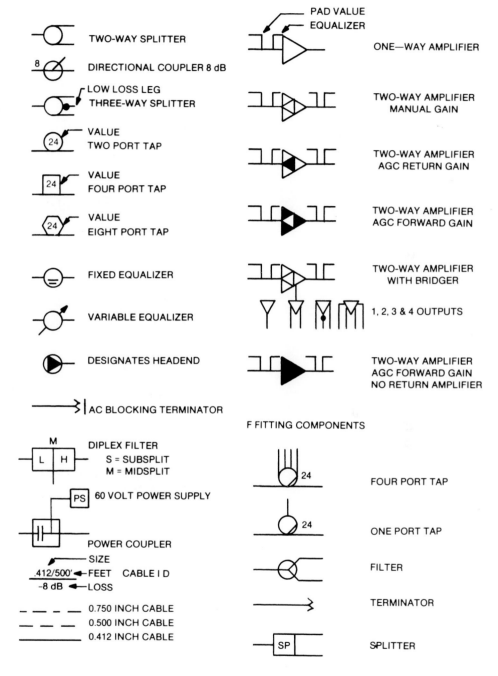

Figure C-1. Broadband Symbols

Appendix D: Frequency Allocations

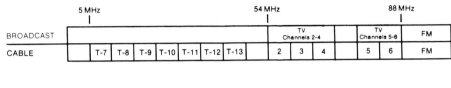

Figure D-1. Frequency Allocation Chart

Table D-1. Headend Channel Assignment Reference Table

FORMER ASSIGNMENT

CHANNEL DESIGNATION	FREQUENCY RANGE MHz
2	54-60
3	60-66
4	66-72
5	76-82
6	82-88
A	120-126
B	126-132
C	132-138
D	138-144
E	144-150
F	150-156
G	156-162
H	162-168
I	168-174
7	174-180
8	180-186
9	186-192
10	192-198
11	198-204
12	204-210
13	210-216
J	216-222
K	222-228
L	228-234
M	234-240
N	240-246
O	246-252
P	252-258
Q	258-264
R	264-270
S	270-276
T	276-282
U	282-288
V	288-294
W	294-300

Incremental assignments are used for non-phaselocked headends and for incrementally related carrier IRC phaselock headends.

Harmonic assignments are used for harmonically related carrier HRC phaselock headends.

INCREMENTAL (IRC) FREQUENCY ASSIGNMENT

CHANNEL DESIGNATION	FREQUENCY RANGE MHz	PICTURE CARRIER MHz	SOUND CARRIER MHz
2	54-60	55.25	59.75
3	60-66	61.25	65.75
4	66-72	67.25	71.75
5*	76-82	77.25	81.75
6*	82-88	83.25	87.75
14I	120-126	121.25	125.75
15I	126-132	127.25	131.75
16I	132-138	133.25	137.75
17I	138-144	139.25	143.75
18I	144-150	145.25	149.75
19I	150-156	151.25	155.75
20I	156-162	157.25	161.75
21I	162-168	163.25	167.75
22I	168-174	169.25	173.75
7	174-180	175.25	179.75
8	180-186	181.25	185.75
9	186-192	187.25	191.75
10	192-198	193.25	197.75
11	198-204	199.25	203.75
12	204-210	205.25	209.75
13	210-216	211.25	215.75
23I	216-222	217.25	221.75
24I	222-228	223.25	227.75
25I	228-234	229.25	233.75
26I	234-240	235.25	239.75
27I	240-246	241.25	245.75
28I	246-252	247.25	251.75
29I	252-258	253.25	257.75
30I	258-264	259.25	263.75
31I	264-270	265.25	269.75
32I	270-276	271.25	275.75
33I	276-282	277.25	281.75
34I	282-288	283.25	287.75
35I	288-294	289.25	293.75
36I	294-300	295.25	299.75
37I	300-306	301.25	305.75
38I	306-312	307.25	311.75
39I	312-318	313.25	317.75
40I	318-324	319.25	323.75
41I	324-330	325.25	329.75
42I	330-336	331.25	335.75
43I	336-342	337.25	341.75
44I	342-348	343.25	347.75
45I	348-354	349.25	353.75
46I	354-360	355.25	359.75
47I	360-366	361.25	365.75
48I	366-372	367.25	371.75
49I	372-378	373.25	377.75
50I	378-384	379.25	383.75
51I	384-390	385.25	389.75
52I	390-396	391.25	395.75
53I	396-402	397.25	401.75
54I*	72-78	73.25	77.75
55I*	78-84	79.25	83.75
56I*	84-90	85.25	89.75
57I	90-96	91.25	95.75
58I	96-102	97.25	101.75
59I	102-108	103.25	107.75
60I	108-114	109.25	113.75
	114-120	115.25	119.75

*Use either 5 and 6 or 54I, 55I, and 56I.

HARMONIC (HRC) FREQUENCY ASSIGNMENT

CHANNEL DESIGNATION	FREQUENCY RANGE MHz	PICTURE CARRIER MHz	SOUND CARRIER MHz
2H	52.75-58.75	54	58.5
3H	58.75-64.75	60	64.5
4H	64.75-70.75	66	70.5
5**	76.75-82.75	78	82.5
6**	82.75-88.75	84	88.5
14H	118.75-124.75	120	124.5
15H	124.75-130.75	126	130.5
16H	130.75-136.75	132	136.5
17H	136.75-142.75	138	142.5
18H	142.75-148.75	144	148.5
19H	148.75-154.75	150	154.5
20H	154.75-160.75	156	160.5
21H	160.75-166.75	162	166.5
22H	166.75-172.75	168	172.5
7H	172.75-178.75	174	178.5
8H	178.75-184.75	180	184.5
9H	184.75-190.75	186	190.5
10H	190.75-196.75	192	196.5
11H	196.75-202.75	198	202.5
12H	202.75-208.75	204	208.5
13H	208.75-214.75	210	214.5
23H	214.75-220.75	216	220.5
24H	220.75-226.75	222	226.5
25H	226.75-232.75	228	232.5
26H	232.75-238.75	234	238.5
27H	238.75-244.75	240	244.5
28H	244.75-250.75	246	250.5
29H	250.75-256.75	252	256.5
30H	256.75-262.75	258	262.5
31H	262.75-268.75	264	268.5
32H	268.75-274.75	270	274.5
33H	274.75-280.75	276	280.5
34H	280.75-286.75	282	286.5
35H	286.75-292.75	288	292.5
36H	292.75-298.75	294	298.5
37H	298.75-304.75	300	304.5
38H	304.75-310.75	306	310.5
39H	310.75-316.75	312	316.5
40H	316.75-322.75	318	322.5
41H	322.75-328.75	324	328.5
42H	328.75-334.75	330	334.5
43H	334.75-340.75	336	340.5
44H	340.75-346.75	342	346.5
45H	346.75-352.75	348	352.5
46H	352.75-358.75	354	358.5
47H	358.75-364.75	360	364.5
48H	364.75-370.75	366	370.5
49H	370.75-376.75	372	376.5
50H	376.75-382.75	378	382.5
51H	382.75-388.75	384	388.5
52H	388.75-394.75	390	394.5
53H	394.75-400.75	396	400.5
54H	70.75-76.75	72	76.5
55H**	76.75-82.75	78	82.5
56H**	82.75-88.75	84	88.5
57H	88.75-94.75	90	94.5
58H	94.75-100.75	96	100.5
59H	100.75-106.75	102	106.5
60H	106.75-112.75	108	112.5
61H	112.75-118.75	114	118.5

**5H and 6H are same as 55H and 56H.

FREQUENCY ASSIGNMENTS FOR SUBSPLIT RETURN CHANNELS ON TWO-WAY SYSTEMS

CHANNEL	FREQUENCY	PICTURE	SOUND
T7	5.75-11.75	7	11.5
T8	11.75-17.75	13	17.5
T9	17.75-23.75	19	23.5
T10	23.75-29.75	25	29.5

Appendix E: RF Calculations

This appendix provides some details on calculations used in the design of RF systems. These details supplement material provided in chapter five on broadband system design. Also, the final section contains a summary list of broadband design equations.

The dBm and dBmV

As previously stated, 0 dBmV = 1 mV. Another commonly-used unit is the *decibel referred to one milliwatt*, abbreviated dBm, and defined as

Number of dBm = $10\log(P/1 \text{ mW})$

where P = power in milliwatts.

This equation provides a positive value when P is greater than 1 mW, and a negative value when P is less than the reference value of 1 mW.

A useful equation relates dBmV and dBm. This equation is based on an assumed impedance value. The common value for CATV systems is 75 Ohms. For a 1 mV drop across a 75-Ohm resistor, the power consumed can be calculated and converted to dBm.

Given 0 dBmV = 1 mV across 75 Ohms,

$P = V^2/R = 1.3(10)^{-8}$ Watts, and in dBm,

$P = 10\log(1.3(10)^{-8})/(10)^{-3})$ dBm

$P = -49$ dBm

Therefore,
0 dBmV = -49 dBm in a 75-Ohm system.

Noise

The basic definition of thermal noise power is

$P_n = kTB$ Watts

where k = $1.38(10)^{-23}$ Joule/°K (Boltzmann's constant)

T = ambient temperature in °K

B = bandwidth in Hertz

When room temperature is assumed (300°K),

$P = 4.1B(10)^{-21}$ Watts (at T=300°K)

Converting this to dBm gives

$P = 10\log(4.1B(10)^{-21}/(10)^{-3})$

$P = -174 + 10\log(B)$ dBm

A noise level in dBmV can also be calculated.

$$E = -174 + 10\log(B) + 49 \text{ dBmV}$$

$$E = -125 + 10\log(B) \text{ dBmV}$$

The minimum noise level (noise floor) for a 4-MHz channel can be found.

$$E_n = -125 + 10\log(4(10)^6)$$

$$E_n = -59 \text{ dBmV}$$

Carrier-to-Noise Ratio

The noise output of a single amplifier, E_{n1} , is

$$E_{n1} = E_{nf} + G + F_0 \text{ dBmV}$$

where E_{nf} = noise floor

G = amplifier gain

F_0 = amplifier noise figure

The carrier-to-noise ratio of one amplifier (C/N_0) is

$$C/N_0 = S - E_{n1}$$
$$= S - E_{nf} - G - F_0$$
$$= -E_{nf} + A - F_0$$

where S = amplifier output level

A = amplifier input level

For example, if noise floor is -59 dBmV, input level is 10 dBmV, and F_0 is 7 dB,

$$C/N_0 = -(-59) + 10 - 7 = 62 \text{ dB}$$

In a cascaded system where N is the number of cascaded amplifiers,

$$\text{System noise figure} = F = F_0 + 10\log(N)$$

$$\text{System } C/N = -E_{nf} + A - F$$
$$= -E_{nf} + A - F_0 - 10\log(N)$$
$$= C/N_0 - 10\log(N)$$

Broadband Design Equations

This section lists some of the equations used in designing broadband networks. Most of these have been covered in the text, and they are listed here together for convenience. Consult appendix B for abbreviations.

A subscript of zero (0) indicates that the parameter is, for example, for an individual amplifier. A subscript of 'c' indicates that the parameter is for a cascade of amplifiers.

dB:	$10\log(P_1/P_2) = 20\log(V_1/V_2)$
dBm:	$10\log(P_1/1\text{ mW})$
dBmV:	$20\log(V_1/1\text{ mV})$
Unity Gain:	Flat Loss + Cable Loss = Amplifier Gain
Rate of change of coaxial cable attenuation with temperature:	1% per 10 degree Fahrenheit change
Carrier Derating:	DCL = VCL - $10\log(NC)$
Noise Floor:	$E_n = -125 + 10\log(B)$ dBmV
Noise Figure of a Cascaded System:	$F_c = F_0 + 10\log(N)$
Noise Floor of a Cascaded System with B = 4MHz:	$E_n = -59 + F_0 + 10\log(N)$ dBmV
C/N of a Single Amplifier:	$C/N_0 =$ Input Level - E_n - F_0
C/N of a Cascaded System:	$C/N_c = C/N_0 - 10\log(N)$
Usable Gain:	Minimum Full Gain - (Module Losses + Reserve Gain)
Maximum Cascaded Amplifier Output Level:	$S_c = S_0 - 10\log(N)$
C/H of a Cascaded System:	$C/H_c = C/H_0 + 20\log(N)$
CTB of a Cascaded System:	$CTB_c = CTB_0 + 20\log(N)$

Appendix F: Test Equipment

This appendix lists test equipment useful for broadband communication networks, including manufacturer's model numbers. Section 6 briefly describes some of the instruments listed here. This list is not comprehensive, nor does it indicate preference for one device over another. It does provide alternate choices in some of the categories.

Table F-1.
Test Equipment for RF Network Certification

Manufacturer	Description	Model
Spectrum Analyzers		
Texscan	Spectrum Analyzer .4-450 MHz	VSM5B
	Digital Storage	DS9
Hewlett Packard	Analyzer .01-450 MHz	8557A, 8558B
	Display	182T
	Option for dBmV Calibration 75 Ohm	001
	Analyzer 100 Hz-1.5 GHz	8568A
	Option 75 Ohm BNC 100 Hz-1500 MHz	001
	Option Handle-Flange Kit	909
	Option Spare Manual	910
	Option Slide Kit	E-10
	IEEE 488 Cable	10631B
Tektronix	Analyzer	462
Tektronix	Analyzer	492
Wavetek		1880
Sweep Generators		
Wavetek	Sweep/Signal Generator 1-500 MHz	1801B
	Pilot Carrier Notches Option	A-7
Wavetek	Sweeper 1-2500 MHz	2002A
	Option Rack Mount	K108
Hewlett Packard	Gen. 100 kHz -990 MHz	8656A
	50 To 75 Ohm Adaptor	11687A
	Option Handle-Flange Kit	909

Table F-1.
Test Equipment for RF Network Certification (Continued)

Manufacturer	Description	Model
Texscan	Sweep Generator 1-1000 MHz	VS-60B
	75-Ohm Impedance	Z Option
	Rack Mount Option	RM Option

Cable Sweep Systems

Manufacturer	Description	Model
Wavetek	Sweep Transmitter 1-450 MHz	1855B
	Notch Filters, Two Adjustable	B-2
	Sweep Analyzer 5-450 MHz	1865B
	Camera with Bezel	C-1
Texscan	SIMO Sweep 1-450 MHz	9551T
	Receiver	9551RS
	Digital Storage Option	

Field Strength Meters

Manufacturer	Description	Model
Texscan	Digital Field Strength Meter	Digitek
	Field Strength Meter	7272
Wavetek	Computerized FSM	SAM III D
	Field Strength Meter	SAM III
	Computerized FSM/Analyzer	SAM IV

Radiation Testers

Manufacturer	Description	Model
Texscan	Bloodhound Transmitter	FDM-1
	Bloodhound Receiver	FDM-2
	Mounting Bracket	MB-2
Wavetek	Calibrated Dipole Antenna	RD-1
Comsonics	Sniffer	S200H-1

Carrier Generators

Manufacturer	Description	Model
Dix Hill	Multi-Channel Generator	5516

Table F-1.
Test Equipment for RF Network Certification (Continued)

Manufacturer	Description	Model
Digital Meters and Frequency Counters		
Fluke	AC/DC Meter	8024B
Hewlett Packard	Frequency Counter	5303B
Variable and Fixed Bandpass Filters		
Texscan	Variable BPF	3U 95/1905XX
Jerrold	Fixed BPF	PBF-*
Wavetek	Variable BPF	PP- 5-110 PP-110-220 PP-220-400
Variable and Fixed Attenuators		
Wavetek	Variable Attenuator	7580.1
Texscan	Switchable Attenuator	SA-70F
	Pad Kit	KFP-75 F Kit
Bridges		
Texscan	Cable Bridges	RCB-3/75
Storage Scope		
Tektronix	Storage Scope	468
Cameras		
Tektronix		C-3013
Wavetek		C-1
Power Meters		
Hewlett Packard		435B
Wavetek		1034A

Appendix G: Tools for Installation and Maintenance

This appendix lists tools that are helpful in installing and maintaining broadband systems. All items included were available when this list was compiled. This list does not indicate a preference for the items listed here over similar items that are not included.

Trunk Cable Tools

Tool	Manufacturer	Model
Cable Trailer 2 Reel w/ 54" dia.	Lemco Tool Corp.	6354
Cable Trailer 2 Reel w/ 54" dia.	Lemco Tool Corp.	5254
Reel Buck	Lemco Tool Corp.	1220
Cable Block	Lemco Tool Corp.	PY-750
Cable Block	Lemco Tool Corp.	M1070-1
Cable Block	General Machine	8093
Cable Block	General Machine	G1315
Corner Block 90 degree	Lemco Tool Corp.	K468J
Corner Block 45 degree	Lemco Tool Corp.	M370J
Cable Chute	Lemco Tool Corp.	S1059
Traction Dynamometer (Tension gage)	Dillon	AX-1A
Pulling Grip (Sling)	Kellems	033-03-010
Loop Former, 0.500 Cable	Q-E Tools & Equip.	R500J
Cable Cutters	Benner-Nawman	UP-B76
Jacket Stripper	Cablematic	JST-500
Stripper, Side Cut	Cablematic	DST-500
Corer	Cable Prep	DCT-500
Corer	Jerrold	CPT-500
Corer	Cablematic	CCT-500
Corer	Lemco Tool Comp.	T-500
Corer (Power)	Lemco Tool Comp.	O-500
Combination Stripper (Basic Power)	Cable Prep	SCT-500
Brake for above		SCT3006
T-Handle for above		TB-3003

Tool	Manufacturer	Model
Center Conductor Cleaner	Cablematic	CC457
Center Conductor Cleaner	Cable Prep	4010

Drop Cable Tools

Tool	Manufacturer	Model
Trimmer	Cablematic	UT6000
Crimper	Cable Prep	HCT-659
Crimper	Cablematic	CR-596
Crimper	Blonder-Tongue	4899
Shield Expander RG-6 Cable	Cablematic	FT-6

Miscellaneous

Tool	Manufacturer	Model
Female "F" to Male "G" Adapter	Jerrold	PGF
Pot Screwdriver	Bourns	Trimpot

Appendix H: Broadband Equipment Suppliers

Full-Line Manufacturers

C-Cor Cable TV Industries
60 Decibel Road
State College, PA 16801
(814) 238-2461

General Instrument Corp.
RF Systems Division
4229 S. Fremont Ave.
Tucson, Arizona 85714
(602) 294-1600
Jerrold Division
Hatboro, PA
(215) 679-4800

Magnavox
CATV Systems, Inc.
133 W. Seneca St.
Manlius, New York 13104
(315) 682-9105

RCA Cablevision System
West Coast
8500 Balboa Bld.
Van Nuys, Calif. 91409
(213) 891-7911/(800) 423-5617
East Coast (800) 345-8104

Scientific Atlanta
Box 105027 Dept. A-R
Atlanta, Georgia 30348
(404) 441-4000

Sylvania
CATV Division
1790 Lee Trevino
Suite 600
El Paso, Texas 79936
(915) 591-3555

Theta-Com Division
122 Cutter Mill Rd.
Great Neck, NY 11021
(800) 528-4066

Support Manufacturers and Distributors

Anixter-Pruzan
18435 Olympic Street
Tukwila, Washington 98124
251-5287
(800) 323-8166

Berk-Tec Cable
Box 60 Rd 1
Reading, Penn 19607
(215) 376-8071

Blonder-Tongue
One Jake Brown Rd.
Old Bridge, NJ 08857
(201) 998-0695

Catel Division
United Scientific Corp.
4800 Patrick Henry Dr.
Santa Clara, CA 95054
(408) 988-7722

Cerro (Capscan Inc.)
Halls Mill Rd
Adedhia, NJ 07710
(201) 462-8700

Com-Scope
RT 1, Box 199A
Catawba, N.C. 28609
(704) 241-3142

Copperweld Corp.
Bi-Metallics Group
2 Robinson Plaza
Pittsburgh, PA 15205
(412) 777-3000

General Cable
P.O. Box 700
Woodbridge, NJ 07095
(201) 636-5500

Gilbert Connector Co.
3700 N. 36 Avenue
Phoenix, Arizona 85019
(800) 528-5567

Oak Communications
CATV Division
Crystal Lake, IL 60014
(815) 459-5000

North Supply
10951 Lakeview Ave.
Lenexa, Kansas 66219
(913) 888-9800

Phasecom Corp
6365 Arizona Circle
Los Angeles, Calif. 90045
(213) 641-3501

Pioneer
3518 Riverside Drive
Columbus, OH 43221
(614) 451-7694

RMS
50 Antin Pl.
Bronx, New York 10462
(800) 223-8312

3M TeleComm Products
Dept. TL81-35
P.O. Box 33600
St. Paul, Minnesota 55133

Times Fiber Communications
Cable TV Division
P.O. Box 384
Wallingford, CT
(203) 265-2361

Tomco Communications Div.
United Scientific Corp.
4800 Patrick Henry Dr.
Santa Clara, CA 95054
(408) 988-7722

Toner Cable Equip.
969 Horsham Rd.
Horsham, PA. 19044
(800) 523-5947

Wavetek
P.O. Box 190
Beech Grove, IN 46107
(317) 787-3332

Appendix H: Broadband Equipment Suppliers (Continued)

Satellite Equipment Manufacturers

A Television Receive Only (TVRO) earth station receives low-power microwave television signals from orbiting communication satellites. The signals are captured with a parabolic antenna, amplified and converted to standard television signals, and then fed to a conventional television distribution system.

Avantek
3175 Bowers Ave.
Santa Clara, CA 95051
(408) 496-6710

Comtech Data Corp.
350 N. Hayden
Scottsdale, AZ 85257
(602) 949-1155

Gardiner Communications
3605 Security Street
Garland, TX 75042
(800) 527-1392

General Instrument Corp.
RF Systems Division
4229 S. Fremont Ave.
Tucson, AZ 85714
(602) 294-1600
Jerrold Division
Hatboro, PA
(215) 679-4800

Hughes Aircraft Comp.
P.O. Box 2999
Torrance, Calif. 90509
(213) 534-2170

Microwave Assoc.
63 3rd Ave.
Burlington, MA 01803
(617) 272-3100

Scientific Atlanta
Box 105027 Dept. A-R
Atlanta, Georgia 30348

SCN
RD. 1, Box 3114
Basking Ridge, NJ 07920
(201) 658-3838

Toner Cable Equipment Inc.
969 Horsham Rd.
Horsham, PA. 19044
(800) 523-5947

Appendix I: System Grounding

Introduction

The problem of ground potential differential between buildings or different areas of a broadband system is often a concern for the installing engineer. This situation occurs when either significantly different loading situations occur in different buildings, or when the actual grounding apparatus for each building is at a different ground potential.

In a single distribution environment such as a single building or factory, a ground grid normally exists. This grid can comprise the structural steel, the plumbing piping, or any other generally available conducting system which is tied to earth through a ground rod or other metallic means. The wire from the grid to the ground is normally #6 copper.

Broadband System Grounding

Broadband systems, just as all other electromagnetic systems, must be grounded. Grounding is important for protection of individuals from shock hazard while using or working on the system, and for proper operation of the active components of the system.

A basic broadband system is grounded at the headend by attaching its power supply to the building's ground. This establishes the initial ground potential of the cable's shield throughout the system.

In all broadband systems, it is recommended that an attachment from each amplifier be made to the ground grid. This minimizes the possible effects of shield currents on power supplies. When this ground attachment is made with hanger clamps to the structural steel, ensure that the paint has been adequately cleaned to make a good metal-to-metal contact.

Grounding individual taps from the trunk cable is not necessary, but can improve power line isolation for the device at the end of the drop. This technique is only suggested for environments where the ground grid is readily accessible and can be used as the mechanical support for the device.

Annual inspection of the trunk cable can identify potential ground failures caused by corrosion, physical damage, or vandalism.

Grounding Between Sites

Broadband systems often connect more than one building or site, and significant ground potential problems might exist. A large difference can cause shield currents on the cable that could degrade the performance of the amplifiers in that area of the system. Reduce these intersite potential differences as much as possible.

▶   Grounding individual amplifiers reduces this problem.
▶   Installing suitable earth rods at the exit and entry points of each site also helps. However, ensure that these earth rod grounds do not function as overall grounds

for the entire site. Information on earth rod techniques is available from manufacturers of this type of equipment, and in references listed in a publication of Copperweld Steel Company.* A megger test of the actual ground is one way to assure a reasonable potential to ground.

Above Ground Exposed Trunks

Intersite trunks which run above ground are exposed to natural energies that are not normally encountered inside a facility. CATV equipment is designed specifically for this environment. Surge protectors in the amplifiers protect the internal circuitry from this type of overload.

▶ Ground every eighth or twelfth support pole with a good earth rod ground to protect the system from the energy transmitted by these forces.

▶ Ground all amplifiers.

▶ Establish a preventive maintenance program to replace the surge protectors annually, especially in areas of high electrical activity.

▶ Periodically inspect the grounds for such problems as corrosion, physical damage, and vandalism.

Ground Loops

Even with a properly designed system using good ground techniques, ground loop problems might occur. These problems are often a result of an inadequate ground grid at the site. The first point of attack should be a thorough survey of the current ground system and of the methods for reducing or eliminating any ground potential differences at the site. If this does not solve the problem, try a sectored approach to ensure that the system ground in each area of the building is adequate. Then ensure that the power system ground potential for the individual devices that are attached in that area are tied together.

It is unusual for a large enough ground potential difference to exist to hamper system performance. A thorough investigation of the system should be conducted before taking these steps to ensure that ground loops are the problem.

Conclusion

While elimination of ground potential differences is the best approach, other techniques are available to eliminate or at least minimize the impact of these problems. The following list identifies the key elements in controlling ground problems in broadband systems.

▶ Ground all amplifiers either directly to the ground grid or to the nearest ground point with #6 copper ground.

---

* "Principles and Practices for Securing Safe, Dependable Grounds by Means of Driven Electrodes," Copperweld Steel Company.

- ▶ For between-site potential differences, first attempt to resolve them using good ground engineering techniques.
- ▶ When between-site potential differences are significant and cannot be eliminated, use properly selected earth grounds at exit and entry points of the sites.
- ▶ Make periodic inspections of the trunk cable and amplifiers to identify potential problems.
- ▶ For overland trunks, use the CATV practice of grounding on every eighth or twelfth pole.
- ▶ For overland trunks, institute a preventive maintenance program for surge protector replacement and cable inspection.
- ▶ For suspected ground loops, first test to ensure that ground loops are really the problem and then use a sectored ground approach.

Appendix J: RF Connector Details

This appendix contains some specific details on RF connectors used in broadband cable systems.

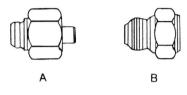

(a) Feed Thru

A   Body with integral mandrel.

B   Locking nut for seizing and retaining cable outer conductor.

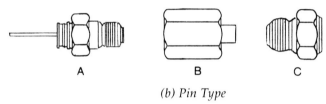

(b) Pin Type

A   Body with cable center conductor seizing pin.

B   Main nut with integral mandrel.

C   Locking nut for seizing and retaining cable outer conductor.

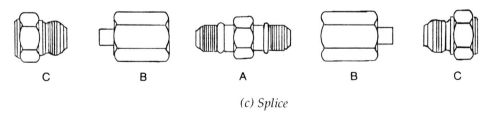

(c) Splice

A   Body with cable center conductor seizing device.

B   Main nut with integral mandrel (two on splice).

C   Locking nut for seizing and retaining cable outer conductor (two on splice).

Figure J-1. Terminology for Connector Parts

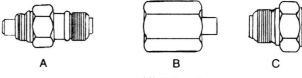

(d) F Female

A   Body with F female port and cable center conductor seizing device.

B   Main nut with integral mandrel.

C   Locking nut for seizing and retaining cable outer conductor.

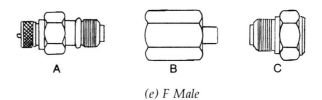

(e) F Male

A   Body with F male connection and cable center conductor seizing device.

B   Main nut with integral mandrel.

C   Locking nut for seizing and retaining cable outer conductor.

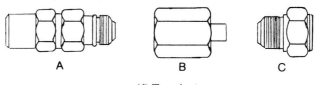

(f) Terminator

A   Body contains RF signal termination and AC power blocking along with cable center conductor seizing devices.

B   Main nut with integral mandrel.

C   Locking nut for seizing and retaining cable outer conductor.

Figure J-1. Terminology for Connector Parts (continued)

The entry port configuration of most equipment (amplifiers, extenders, taps, etc.) used with coaxial cable has the following dimensions.

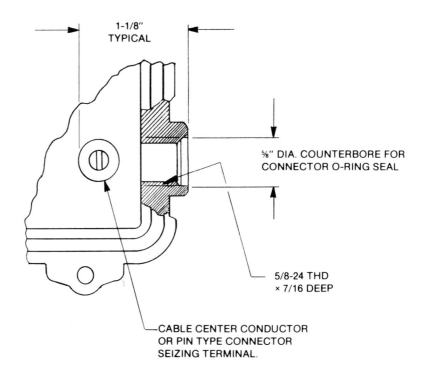

Entry connectors, both feed thru and pin type, are manufactured to be compatible with this port design.

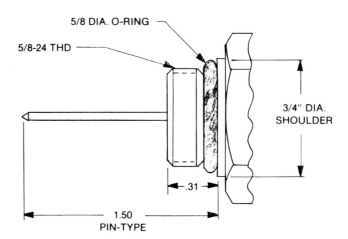

Figure J-2. Connector/Equipment Interface

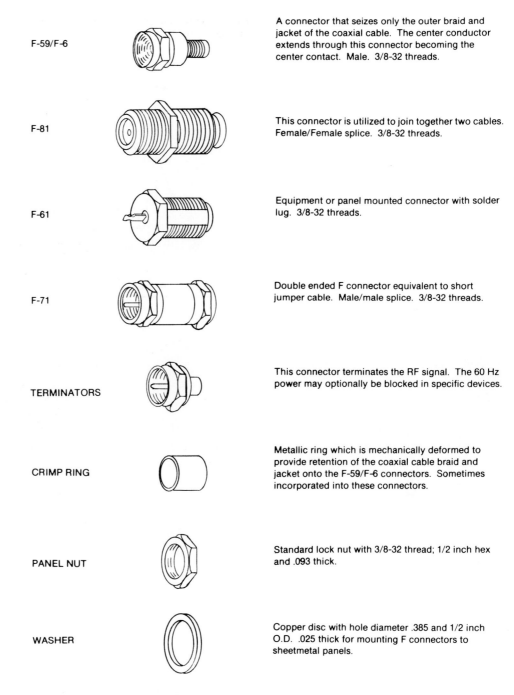

F-59/F-6 — A connector that seizes only the outer braid and jacket of the coaxial cable. The center conductor extends through this connector becoming the center contact. Male. 3/8-32 threads.

F-81 — This connector is utilized to join together two cables. Female/Female splice. 3/8-32 threads.

F-61 — Equipment or panel mounted connector with solder lug. 3/8-32 threads.

F-71 — Double ended F connector equivalent to short jumper cable. Male/male splice. 3/8-32 threads.

TERMINATORS — This connector terminates the RF signal. The 60 Hz power may optionally be blocked in specific devices.

CRIMP RING — Metallic ring which is mechanically deformed to provide retention of the coaxial cable braid and jacket onto the F-59/F-6 connectors. Sometimes incorporated into these connectors.

PANEL NUT — Standard lock nut with 3/8-32 thread; 1/2 inch hex and .093 thick.

WASHER — Copper disc with hole diameter .385 and 1/2 inch O.D. .025 thick for mounting F connectors to sheetmetal panels.

Figure J-3. F Connector Types and Parts

Appendix K: Bibliography

Some of these publications might be out of print, but can often be found on the dusty shelves of the local electronic distributor or book store. Many texts can be located in the technical section of good public or university libraries.

Ameco, Inc., *Cable Installation Handbook,* Milwaukee, McGrawEdison Power Systems Division, #67100.

Baum, Robert E. and Theodore B., *101 Questions & Answers About CATV & MATV,* Indianapolis, Indiana, Howard W. Sams & Co. Inc., 1968. #20655.

Beever, Jack, *Engineer's Guide To Specifications For Multiple Television Distribution Systems,* Philadelphia, Jerrold Electronics Corporation, 1966.

Buckwalter, Len, *99 Ways To Improve Your TV Reception,* Indianapolis, Howard W. Sams & Co. Inc., 1969. #20708.

Camps, Albert, and Markum, Joseph A., *Microwave Primer,* Indianapolis, Howard W. Sams & Co. Inc., 1965. #MMC-1.

Cantor, Lon, *How To Select And Install Antennas,* New York, Hayden Book Company, 1969. #0786.

Cantor, Lon, *Planning & Installing Master Antenna TV Systems,* New York, John F. Rider Publisher, Inc., 1965. #0388.

Cooper, Bernarr, *ITFS Instructional Television Fixed Service (2500 Megahertz) What It Is — How To Plan,* Washington, D.C., National Education Association, 1967.

Cooper, Robert B., Jr., *CATV System Maintenance,* Blue Ridge Summit, Pa., Tab Books, 1970. #T-82.

Cooper, Robert B., Jr., *CATV System Management & Operation,* Blue Ridge Summit, Pa., Tab Books, 1966, #T100.

Copperweld Bimetallics Group, *Practical Grounding,* Pittsburgh, Pa.

Cunningham, John E., *Cable Television,* Second Edition, Indianapolis, Howard W. Sams & Co., Inc., 1980. #21755.

Darr, Jack, *Eliminating Man-Made Interference,* Indianapolis, Howard W. Sams & Co., Inc., 1960. #MMD-1.

Diamond, Robert M., *A Guide To Instructional Television,* New York, McGraw-Hill Book Company, 1964.

Editors of "Electronic Technical/Dealer", *A Practical Guide To MATV/CATV System Design & Service,* Blue Ridge Summit, Pa., Tab Books, 1974. #731.

Elroy, Hansen & Lawrence, Paul, *Home TV-FM Antennas,* Indianapolis, Howard W. Sams & Co., Inc., 1974. #21076.

FCC Rules and Regulations, *Technical Standards for CATV,* Section 15, Subpart K, Sections 76-601 to 76-617.

Hewlett Packard, *Cable Television System Measurements Handbook,* Santa Rosa, Ca., Hewlett-Packard Co., 1977. #5955-8509.

Kamen, Ira, *Questions And Answers About Pay TV*, Indianapolis, Howard W. Sams & Co., Inc., 1973. #20971.

Kamen, Ira and Doundoulakis, George, *Scatter Propagation*, Indianapolis, Howard W. Sams & Co., Inc., 1956. #SPK-1.

Kuecken, John A., *Antennas And Transmission Lines*, Indianapolis, Howard W. Sams Co., Inc., 1969. #20716.

Lytel, Allen, *ABC's of Antennas*, Indianapolis, Howard W. Sams Co., Inc., 1966. #AAL-1.

Lytel, Allen, *Microwave Test & Measurement Techniques*, Indianapolis, Howard W. Sams Co., Inc., 1964. #MIL-1.

Lytel, Allen, *UHF Television Antennas And Converters*, New York, John F. Rider Publisher, Inc., 1953. #153.

Mivec, F. Johnathan, *Microwave Systems Fundamentals*, Indianapolis, Howard W. Sams & Co. Inc., 1963. #MSM-1.

National Cable Television Association, *Standards of Good Engineering Practices for Measurements on Cable Television Systems, Distribution System*, Washington, D.C., NCTA, 1977. #008-0477.

Pawlowski, Allen, *MATV Systems Handbook-Design, Installation & Maintenance*, Blue Ridge Summit, Pa., Tab Books, 1973. #657.

Ray, Verne M., *CATV Operator's Handbook*, Blue Ridge Summit, Pa., Tab Books, 1967.

Rheinfelder, William A., *CATV System Engineering*, Blue Ridge Summit, Pa., Tab Books, 1970. #298.

Salvati, M.J., *RF Interference Handbook*, New York, Sony Corporation of America, Technical Publications Department, 1977.

Salvati, M.J., *TV Antennas And Signal Distribution Systems*, Indianapolis, Howard W. Sams & Co. Inc., 1979. #21584.

Sands, Leo G., *Installing TV & FM Antennas*, Blue Ridge Summit, Pa., Tab Books, 1974. #636.

Shrock, Clifford B., *No Loose Ends, The Tektronix Proof-of-Performance Program for CATV*, Tektronix Application Note, 1973. #26W-4889.

Simons, Ken, *Technical Handbook For CATV Systems*, Third edition, Hatboro, Pa., General Instrument Corporation, Jerrold Division, 1968. #436-001-01.

Television Publications, Inc., *National Standards for CATV Systems, Graphic Symbols*, Oklahoma City, Oklahoma 73107.

Wortman, Leon A., *Closed Circuit Television Handbook*, Indianapolis, Howard W. Sams & Co. Inc., 1964. #CLC-1.

Appendix L: dBmV-to-Voltage Conversion Chart

Table L-1.
dBmV/Voltage Conversion Chart

dBmV	μV	dBmV	μV	dBmV	μV
−40	10	0	1,000	40	100,000
−39	11	1	1,100	41	110,000
−38	13	2	1,300	42	130,000
−37	14	3	1,400	43	140,000
−36	16	4	1,600	44	160,000
−35	18	5	1,800	45	180,000
−34	20	6	2,000	46	200,000
−33	22	7	2,200	47	220,000
−32	25	8	2,500	48	250,000
−31	28	9	2,800	49	280,000
−30	32	10	3,200	50	320,000
−29	36	11	3,600	51	360,000
−28	40	12	4,000	52	400,000
−27	45	13	4,500	53	450,000
−26	50	14	5,000	54	500,000
−25	56	15	5,600	55	560,000
−24	63	16	6,300	56	630,000
−23	70	17	7,000	57	700,000
−22	80	18	8,000	58	800,000
−21	90	19	9,000	59	900,000
−20	100	20	10,000	60	1.0 volt
−19	110	21	11,000	61	1.1 volts
−18	130	22	13,000	62	1.2 volts
−17	140	23	14,000	63	1.4 volts
−16	160	24	16,000	64	1.6 volts
−15	180	25	18,000	65	1.8 volts
−14	200	26	20,000	66	2.0 volts
−13	220	27	22,000	67	2.2 volts
−12	250	28	25,000	68	2.5 volts
−11	280	29	28,000	69	2.8 volts
−10	320	30	32,000	70	3.2 volts
−9	360	31	36,000	71	3.6 volts
−8	400	32	40,000	72	4.0 volts
−7	450	33	45,000	73	4.5 volts
−6	500	34	50,000	74	5.0 volts
−5	560	35	56,000	75	5.6 volts
−4	630	36	63,000	76	6.3 volts
−3	700	37	70,000	77	7.0 volts
−2	800	38	80,000	78	8.0 volts
−1	900	39	90,000	79	9.0 volts
−0	1,000	40	100,000	80	10.0 volts

Definition of dBmV: 0 dBmV = 1,000 μV across 75 ohms.

Index

Index

N

narrow bandwidth advantages, 74
narrow bandwidth carrier levels, 72ff
narrow bandwidth data signals, 37
NC (number of carriers), 72
network, 15
network architecture and topology, 63
network breakdown, 38
network design, 19
network design, broadband 62ff
network elements, 12
network examples, 9
network failure, 38
network manager, 62
network RF test point, 93
network size, 9
network, troubleshooting, 51
networks, connecting, 33
node, 13
noise at a splitter/combiner, 77-78
noise calculations, 130
noise figure, 47, 50, 75, 84
noise figure, typical, 82
noise floor, 21, 75, 82, 84
noise floor, defined 75
noise level, 40, 75ff
noise spike, 79
noise, system, 81
noise, thermal, 75
non-amplified system, 107
nontranslated devices, 93
number of carriers (NC), 72

O

office of the future, 7
office outlet levels, 98
one-way service, 40
one-way system, 16, 31
one-way trunk, 33
operating current and voltage, amplifier, 52
operating experience, 9
operating window, 84
outbound, 15, 31
outbound cable, 110
outlet, 9, 13, 38-39, 43, 51, 60, 69-70
outlet, checking an, 113

outlet drop cable problems, 112
outlet, dual cable system, 32, 39
outlet level, 24
outlet levels, industrial, 98
outlet levels, office, 98
outlet signal amplitude, 71
outlets, single and dual cable systems, 39
output level, 47, 84
output level, amplifier, 84
output level margin, 86
output ports, 112
output side, amplifier, 49
outside noise sources, 82
overcompensation, 48, 79
overdrive, 72
overhead cable installation, 44
overloading amplifiers, 37
overtightening, 111

P

packet communication unit, 29, 66
pad selection, 108
passive component failures, 112
passive components, 18, 53ff, 64
passive loss, 23, 53
passive taps, 20
patch panel, 93
path layout, 38
path loss, forward, 71
path, return, 40
performance test, 104
periodic maintenance, 87
physical inspection, 87
physical layout, 68-69
physical topology, 12
picture quality for C/N values, 77
pilot carrier signal, 79
point-to-point RF modems, 66
pole mounting, 43
ports, 57
power, 20
power, cable, 19
power capacity of amplifiers, 37
power combiner, 51, 93
power distribution, 51
power, emergency, 87

U

underground cable, 48
underground installations, 54
unidirectional, 4, 14
unity gain criterion, 22
upgrading, 16
upgrading a network, 39
usable gain, 80
usable gain, amplifier, 47
user outlets, 13
uses, business, 6
uses, educational, 8
uses, industrial, 7
utility, 3
utility, information, 63

V

valves, 20
variable equalizers, 50
variation of cable attenuation, frequency, 45

variation of cable attenuation, temperature, 46
VCL, 72
vendor independence, 8
ventilation, 44
VHF television channels, 28
video applications, 39
video bandpass, 72
video carrier level (VCL), 72
video reference level, 70
visual carrier signal, 25
voltage, 20
voltage dependent, amplifier, 52
voltage levels, 21

W

Wang Laboratories, 31
water delivery system, 20
work-at-home, 7